*New Chapters in the
History of Greek Literature*

New Chapters in the History of Greek Literature

RECENT DISCOVERIES IN GREEK POETRY
AND PROSE OF THE FOURTH AND
FOLLOWING CENTURIES B.C.

EDITED BY

J. U. POWELL AND E. A. BARBER

Biblo & Tannen
New York
1974

880.9
P88n
1974

Originally Published 1921
Reprinted 1974
With the Permission of
The Clarendon Press

by

Biblo & Tannen Booksellers & Publishers, Inc.
63 Fourth Avenue   New York, N.Y. 10003

Library of Congress Cataloging in Publication Data

Powell, John Undershell, 1865-   ed.
    New chapters in the history of Greek literature.

    Reprint of the 1921 ed. published by Clarendon
Press, Oxford.
    1. Greek literature--Addresses, essays, lectures.
I. Barber, Eric Arthur, 1888-   joint ed.
II. Title.
PA3061.P6 1974b   880'.9'001   74-2062
ISBN 0-8196-0286-8

45-4056

Printed in U.S.A. by
NOBLE OFFSET PRINTERS, INC.
New York, N.Y. 10003

PREFACE

When Mr. Evelyn Abbott wrote with truth in his glowing preface to *Hellenica* (1879), 'We have not done with the Hellenes yet . . .; we have not entered into full possession of the inheritance bequeathed to us', he had in his mind, as he goes on to show, the significance of Greek history and literature, rather than additions to our knowledge due to the discovery of new texts. But although some years were to elapse, his words in another sense have come true. Twelve years afterwards, in 1891, a new epoch of Greek scholarship opened, not only in this country, but in others; for in that year Professor Mahaffy published the first part of the Petrie Papyri which Professor Flinders Petrie had discovered, containing parts of the *Phaedo* of Plato and of the *Antiope* of Euripides, with fragments of Homer, and other pieces; while the Trustees of the British Museum published Aristotle's 'Athenian Constitution', the Mimes of Herondas, who had been hitherto little more than a name, and part of a new speech by Hyperides. Other discoveries followed; six years later, in 1897, the British Museum published the Odes of Bacchylides, and Messrs. Grenfell and Hunt began the series of discoveries at Oxyrhynchus, the publication of which has proceeded up to the present time. Nor must we forget the important accessions from Inscriptions, such as Isyllus of Epidaurus, and the Hymns of Aristonous and others from Delphi.

It is a misfortune to British scholarship that our histories of Greek Literature, with the exception of Professor Mahaffy's books, stop short with the death of Demosthenes, or treat but briefly of the succeeding centuries. We have nothing like the admirable and comprehensive history of MM. Croiset in France. But although the following pages do not profess to give an account of what is called 'the Alexandrian age' of Greek Literature, we hope that, through the new texts which are treated of in them, they will make large additions to our knowledge of the literature during the fourth and following centuries B.C. up to the beginning of the Roman Era in the Greek world (which may conveniently be dated with the formation of the Province of Achaea after the capture of Corinth in 146 B.C.), and may encourage future writers on the subject to lengthen their range. The number of the additions is surprisingly large.

We may also hope that the Oxford and Continental Papyri which have been, or may be, recovered from Egypt and Herculaneum, will provide new material even more valuable and interesting than that which is presented to the reader, in most cases for the first time, in the following pages.

A revised text of most of the discoveries mentioned in the first and second sections of the table of contents is ready for the press.

A convenient summary of Greek Papyri and their

contribution to classical literature is given by Sir F. G. Kenyon in a paper bearing that title, published by the Cambridge University Press in 1918, and also printed in the *Journal of Hellenic Studies*, vol. xxxix, pp. 1 sqq.; and in his article 'Greek Papyri and Recent Discoveries', *Quarterly Review*, vol. 208, p. 333. See also a paper by Professor Grenfell on ' The Value of Papyri for the Textual Criticism of Extant Greek Authors', *Journal of Hellenic Studies*, vol. xxxix, pp. 16 sqq. The fullest account is given in the various numbers of *Archiv für Papyrusforschung*, edited by U. Wilcken, and by W. Schubart in *Einführung in die Papyruskunde*, Berlin, 1918. There is no collection of the new poems which have been preserved in Inscriptions.

It may be added, that, while exercising a general supervision over the articles, we have allowed to each contributor the expression of his individual opinions.

J. U. P.
E. A. B.

Oxford,
May 1921.

ERRATA

PAGE

19, three lines from the end of the Greek text, *read* κέντρα τεῖδ'

29, line 11, *for* Olivi i *read* Olivieri

36, last line but one of the text, *for* first *read* second

48, last line but one of text, *for* Macedonia *read* Thessaly

50, seven lines from foot of text, *for* Itana *read* Itanos

55, note 3, *for* 679 B *read* 697 C

56, last line of text, *for* A. D. 100 *read* 100 B. C.

69, line 2, *for* (the Guardians) *read* (the Arbitrants)

70, note 2, line 3, *for* πολλῶν *read* πολλοῦ

95, note 6, line 2, *for* τούτων καλὴ *read* τούτου νῦν καλὴ

108, last reference in the last line, *for* xxxiv *read* xxxiii

146, last word, *for* whom *read* who

Powell and Barber

TABLE OF CONTENTS

I. THE MORALISTS

II. LYRIC POETRY

§ 1. *Hieratic: The Paean, The Hymn.*

CONTRIBUTORS

ANONYMOUS.

E. A. BARBER, M.A., Fellow, Tutor and Sub-Rector of Exeter College.

C. J. ELLINGHAM, M.A., formerly Scholar of St. John's College, Master at Dulwich College.

F. W. HALL, M.A., Fellow and Tutor of St. John's College.

L. C. ST. A. LEWIS, formerly Scholar of St. John's College.

The Rev. T. W. LUMB, M.A., formerly Scholar of Jesus College, Master at Merchant Taylors' School.

GILBERT MURRAY, D.Litt., Regius Professor of Greek.

J. U. POWELL, M.A., Fellow and Senior Tutor of St. John's College.

The Rev. G. C. RICHARDS, B.D., Fellow and Senior Tutor of Oriel College.

J. L. STOCKS, M.A , D.S.O., Fellow and Tutor of St. John's College.

The Rev. E. M. WALKER, M.A., Fellow and Senior Tutor of Queen's College.

New Chapters in the
History of Greek Literature

I

THE MORALISTS

DURING the last twenty years the laborious researches of scholars and the happy discovery of certain illuminating papyri have thrown much light on the popular philosophy of the Hellenistic period. The great importance in this sphere of the so-called $\Delta\iota\alpha\tau\rho\iota\beta\dot{\eta}$ has been generally recognized, and a very considerable store of philosophic commonplaces has been collected from later writers, Greek and Roman, and derived with much probability from the popular teachers of this age. It is admitted that among these teachers the most conspicuous were the Cynic missionaries; the type which we find fully developed under the Roman Empire, but which was already represented in the third century B. C. At the same time it is a mistake to claim all this moralizing for the Cynic school. By the third century many of the ideas which, in the days of Antisthenes or even Diogenes, were peculiar to that sect, had become the common property of all men, and were given literary expression by authors of any or no philosophic school. Of the two poets to be considered in this section Cercidas is proved by external and internal evidence to have been a Cynic, while Phoenix appears to be no more affected by Cynic ideas than any man who wrote as a popular philosopher in that age was bound to be. In other words, the contempt for the ordinary standards of civilized life, the criticism of society, the exaltation of the poor and oppressed, ideas which the Cynics had been the first to introduce into Greek literature, became in time the weapons of any democrat with a turn for satire who was against the established order, or for the nonce pretended to be against it.

The Diatribe proper is a prose composition, being originally the form which the philosophers of the streets gave to their popular addresses. The topic of each is generally some well-

worn theme, such as Wealth, Death, Marriage, &c., but the
writer contrives to give it life by vivid metaphors, witty
anecdotes, striking antitheses, or apt quotations from the poets.
It was inevitable that the genre should make its influence felt
in the poetry of the age, and as a matter of fact we can point
to Cynic Tragedies, Satiric Elegies, Epic Parodies, and
Iambic Moralizings, all of them affected in various degrees
by the prose diatribe. It is by the light of these facts that
we must interpret the new material.

Cercidas.

Before the publication of Volume VIII of the *Oxyrhynchus
Papyri* Cercidas was represented by nine fragments only.[1]
The Papyrus (No. 1082) published in that volume by Professor
Hunt gives us about seventy new fragments, but of these only
four or five are large enough to be appreciated. That Cercidas
was a Cynic had been inferred from the tone of the existing
fragments and from a reference in Athenaeus,[2] an inference
which is now confirmed by the subscription at the end of
Fr. 4.[3] Over his date the division of opinion had been greater.
The name Cercidas occurs several times in the inscriptions
of Arcadia. Wilamowitz[4] gives reasons for thinking that the
family bearing this name belonged originally to Methydrion,
a small place in Arcadia, which was eventually absorbed in
Megalopolis. However that may be, it is certain that the
two best-known men of the name were in fact politicians
of Megalopolis. The earlier of them was a contemporary of
Demosthenes, and is accused by him of betraying Megalopolis
to Philip ;[5] the second was a supporter of Aratus, and com-
manded the Megalopolitan contingent at the battle of Sellasia.[6]
Now Stephanus of Byzantium[7] describes Megalopolis as the
city of Cercidas ἄριστος νομοθέτης καὶ μελιάμβων ποιητής. It
seems therefore probable that our poet was one of the two

---

[1] Bergk, *Poet. Lyr.* ii, pp. 513–15.   [2] Athen. viii. 347 e.
[3] Κερκίδα Κυνὸς μελίαμβοι.
[4] *Sitzungsb. preuss. Akad.*, 1918, pp. 1138 sqq.
[5] *De Cor.* 295.   [6] Polyb. ii. 48–50, 65.
[7] Steph. Byz. Μεγαλόπολις.

statesmen just mentioned. Meineke and Leo wished to identify him with the fourth-century politician, but the reference in Fr. 2 (Bergk) to the death of Diogenes (323 B. C.) as a not very recent event was against this ; and now, as Hunt points out, the allusions to the Stoic Zeno and his pupil Sphaerus make it certain that the poet belonged to the third century, and render it probable that he should be placed in the second half of it. Νομοθεσία such as that attributed to him by Stephanus might be called for at any period in a state's history, and it has been plausibly conjectured that Cercidas's legislation followed Lydiades' voluntary surrender of his tyranny in 235 B. C., when Megalopolis joined the Achaean League. The poet then is to be identified with the statesman and general mentioned by Polybius. Further proof of the correctness of this dating is afforded by the social conditions reflected in the new fragments. In particular the first poem in Fr. 1 is clearly written at a time when the property question absorbed the public interest ; and the age of Aratus and Cleomenes was, as is well known, such a time. Throughout Greece the economic pressure was responsible for endless revolutionary movements which aimed at a cancelling of debts and redistribution of wealth. The Achaean League, with Aratus at its head, represented the property-owning classes of the Peloponnese ; while Sparta, where the inequality of wealth was most glaring, became first under Agis and then under Cleomenes the champion of the Social Revolution. It is true that Cercidas's profession of the Cynic faith and the sentiments which he expresses in his Meliambs are not quite what we should expect from the man described by Polybius as the πατρικὸς ξένος of Aratus. But we must remember that adherence to a philosophic school was in some cases merely formal.[1] Most of the Cynics, both in Hellenistic times and under the Roman Empire, were of the ' poor philosopher ' type ; but there was nothing absurd in a politician with a turn for the unconventional professing himself a follower of Diogenes. At the same time it may be wrong to take Cercidas's philosophy

---

[1] Wilamowitz compares it with the modern membership of a church !

too lightly. That there were idealists even among the associates of Aratus is proved by the example of Lydiades, the
fellow-countryman of Cercidas, and perhaps the latter's attack
on the grasping and vicious rich in Fr. 1 was meant as a warning to his own party to mend their ways before it was too late.
Yet in the end Cercidas's class-consciousness seems to have
prevailed over his sympathies for the poor ; for at the critical
period when Cleomenes was carrying all before him he
consented to go as one of Aratus's confidential emissaries to
Antigonus, and in the roundabout way described by Polybius
to solicit his intervention on behalf of the Achaean League.
No doubt the Philo-Macedonian policy of his city and family
caused him to be selected for the task. Cercidas's action must
in part have been dictated by patriotic considerations.
Cleomenes and the party which he led were at this time
abandoning their social reforms for a career of aggressive
imperialism—a phenomenon not unknown to-day—and Megalopolis, *nimium vicina* to Sparta, was in a position of considerable danger, as was shown all too clearly by Cleomenes'
destruction of the city a few years later (222 B. C.).

Cercidas wrote Iambi and Meliambi. Of the former only
one line survives in a quotation[1] from Athenaeus, but from it
we see that in this case, as often, ' Iambi ' means Choliambi or
Scazons. The fragment is of no particular interest in itself,
but it at least demonstrates that Cercidas contributed to the
third-century revival of the satiric Iambus. His poetic fame
however really rested on the Meliambi, and all the new
fragments belong to this class. The meaning of the word
' Meliambus ' is not quite certain. According to some scholars
it denotes a species of verse where the form is lyrical but the
content ' iambic ', i. e. satiric : Maas,[2] however, refers it to the
metre only, supposing that the prefix $\mu\epsilon\lambda$- represents the
dactylic portion of Cercidas's measures, but this seems scarcely
likely. No other writer of Meliambi is known to us.

The fragments preserved by Stobaeus and others do not call
for lengthy notice. The most famous is the description of

---

[1] Athen. xii. 554 d.   [2] *Berl. Phil. Woch.*, 1911, pp. 1214 sqq.

Diogenes' death with the pun on his name in the concluding
lines:[1]

$$Z\alpha\nu\grave{o}s \ \gamma\acute{o}\nu os \ \mathring{\eta}s \ \gamma\grave{a}\rho \ \mathring{a}\lambda\alpha\theta\acute{\epsilon}\omega s$$
$$o\mathring{v}\rho\acute{a}\nu\iota\acute{o}s \ \tau\epsilon \ \kappa\acute{v}\omega\nu.$$

Cercidas's adaptation[2] of the saying of Epicharmus $\nu o\hat{v}s \ \mathring{o}\rho\hat{\eta}$
$\kappa\alpha\grave{\iota} \ \nu o\hat{v}s \ \mathring{a}\kappa o\acute{v}\epsilon\iota$[3] is interesting. This saying had become
proverbial, and both before Cercidas's time and after received
many different applications. Cercidas's meaning would seem
to be as follows. True seeing and true hearing can only be
accomplished by means of $\nu o\hat{v}s$. Therefore it behoves a man
to abstain from dissipation and luxurious living lest $\nu o\hat{v}s$ be
unable to fulfil its functions. This adaptation of a text from
an earlier poet is quite in the Cynic style, and finds a parallel
in the quotations from Homer and Euripides contained in the
fragment from Oxyrhynchus. One fragment[4] has curiously
enough been preserved by the Greek Father, St. Gregory
Nazianzen, who gives Cercidas the designation $\mathring{o} \ \phi\acute{\iota}\lambda\tau\alpha\tau os$.
Whether St. Gregory was attracted by the Cynic poet's hostility
to polytheism or by his satirical powers is unknown. Unfortunately the passage is very corrupt; but the gist of it would
seem to be that the rich man's food, no less than that of the
poor man, eventually finds its way $\epsilon\mathring{\iota}s \ \beta v\theta\acute{o}\nu$, the interpretation
of which phrase may be left to the reader.

We turn now to the new fragments. Of these Fr. 1 is far
the most important. It contains part of two separate poems,
the break being clearly marked in the papyrus. The first
poem deals with the unequal distribution of wealth, and the
question which this raises of a Divine Providence. Cercidas
inveighs against two classes of men on whom wealth is wasted,
the *avare*, whom he quaintly terms $\mathring{\rho}v\pi o\kappa\iota\beta\delta o\tau\acute{o}\kappa\omega\nu$[5] and
$\tau\epsilon\theta\nu\alpha\kappa o\chi\alpha\lambda\kappa\acute{\iota}\delta\alpha s$,[6] and the spendthrift, who is more obscurely
castigated as $\pi\alpha\lambda\iota\nu\epsilon\kappa\chi v\mu\epsilon\nu\acute{\iota}\tau\alpha s$.[7] He asks why Heaven does

[1] For the order of words see von Arnim, *Wien. Stud.* xxxiv, pp. 1 sqq.
[2] Fr. 4, Bergk.
[3] Epicharmus, Fr. 249, Kaibel. [4] Fr. 7, Bergk.
[5] Apparently = 'dirty cheating usurer'. Arnim compares $\mathring{\rho}v\pi\alpha\rho\acute{\iota}\alpha$ =
sordes in Teles. C. favours the termination -$\omega\nu$.
[6] Arnim paraphrases $\mathring{o} \ \tau\epsilon\theta\nu\eta\kappa\acute{o}\tau\alpha \ \tau\grave{o}\nu \ \chi\alpha\lambda\kappa\grave{o}\nu \ \mathring{\epsilon}\chi\omega\nu$.
[7] $\pi\acute{a}\lambda\iota\nu$ seems to suggest that the spendthrift cannot *retain* his wealth.
Comp. $\mathring{\epsilon}\xi\epsilon\mu\acute{\epsilon}\sigma\alpha\iota$ in same fragment.

not empty these men of their ' swinish wealth ' and distribute
it among the poor, who would then have the wherewithal to
meet their 'bits of expense'. Can it be, he proceeds, that
Justice is blind like a mole ; that Phaethon (i. e. the sun) sees
crookedly with a single eyeball, and that the brightness of
Themis has been dimmed ? If we accept this apology, why
continue to regard as gods creatures that have neither hearing
nor opening for vision? Arrived thus far in his argument,
Cercidas then turns to deal with the Homeric evidence in
favour of a Divine Providence, evidence which is only obtained
by a characteristically Cynic perversion of the well-known
passages where Homer describes the Scales of Zeus.[1] The
papyrus is mutilated at this point but the general sense is
plain.

$$καὶ \ μὰν \ τὸ \ τάλαντον \ ὁ \ σεμνὸς$$
$$ἀστεροπαγερέτας \ μέσσον \ τὸν \ Ὄλυμπον \ (ἔχων)^{2}$$
$$ὀρθὸν \ (τιταίνει)^{3} \ καὶ \ νένευκεν \ οὐδαμῆ·$$
$$καὶ \ τοῦθ' \ Ὅμηρος \ εἶπεν \ ἐν \ Ἰλιάδι·$$
$$ῥέπει \ δ', \ ὅταν \ αἴσιμον \ ἆμαρ,$$
$$ἀνδράσι \ κυδαλίμοις.$$

i. e. according to Cercidas the falling scale means the bestowal
of wealth, while in Homer of course it forebodes disaster or
death. The poet has no difficulty in disposing of this argument ; it is refuted by the facts of his personal experience,

$$πῶς \ οὖν \ ἐμὶν \ οὔποτ' \ ἔρεψεν$$
$$ὀρθὸς \ ὢν \ ζυγοστάτας ;$$
$$τὰ \ δ' \ ἔσχατα \ βρύτια \ Μυσῶν^{4}—$$
$$ἄζομαι \ δὲ \ θὴν \ λέγειν$$
$$ὅσον \ παταγεῖ^{5} \ τὸ \ παρ' \ αὐτοῖς$$
$$τῶ \ Διὸς \ πλαστίγγιον.$$

After that there is nothing left to be said. If the son of
Cronos who begat all of us has been revealed as a father to some,
and a stepfather to others, it is useless to apply to other sons of
Heaven, and the wise man will leave these problems to the

---

[1] Θ 70-2 : X 209-12.　　　　[2] ἔχων *supplevit* Wilamowitz.
[3] τιταίνει *supplevit* Wilamowitz.
[4] *sic* Arnim. For βρύτια see L. & S.　τα δ' ἐσχᾶτᾱ φρυγια μυσων Pap.
with βρυγια in margin.
[5] παταγεῖ Wilamowitz : . . . . γει Pap.

astrologers (μετεωροκόποι), who are not likely to have any
difficulty in finding a solution. Meanwhile,

> ἀμὶν δὲ Παιὰν καὶ Μετάδως¹ μελέτω,
> θεὸς γὰρ αὖτα
> καὶ Νέμεσις κατὰ γᾶν.

'But let Paean and Giving be our care, for she (i. e. Giving)
is a goddess and a Nemesis still present on earth.'

Μετάδως, the certain correction of Wilamowitz, is of course
a new formation from μεταδιδόναι on the analogy of Δὼς ἀγαθή
in Hesiod (*Opera*, 356), and the Hesiodic phrase has been
written in the margin of the Papyrus by some intelligent com-
mentator.   Cercidas clearly means that care for the sick and
charity to the poor ought to be the principles governing one's
life, and with a play on the etymology of the word (νέμειν =
μεταδιδόναι) he calls this charity a Nemesis still walking the
earth, whatever may have happened to the Nemesis of the old
theology.   Nevertheless the connexion of thought is not
obvious.   Up to this point—we must presume by a convenient
fiction—Cercidas has made himself the spokesman of the poor
and has reckoned himself one of them.   By ἀμίν then he
ought again to refer to the poor, who on this view are exhorted
not to worry about life's undoubted inequalities, but to practise
good works among themselves.   But this interpretation agrees
very ill with the sentence which immediately follows,

> μέσφ' οὖν ὁ δαίμων
> οὔρια φυσιάει, τιμᾶτε ταύταν.

The poor could not be called on to honour the goddess 'while
the deity blows favourably'.   We must then conclude that
from ἀμὶν δὲ Παιάν onwards Cercidas drops the pretence of
speaking as a poor man, and appeals to his fellows of the
wealthy class to show more humanity in dealing with their
inferiors.   The last lines of the poem are unhappily not complete, but, if we accept the ingenious suggestions of von Arnim,
it would seem that Cercidas followed up his exhortation by
a warning of what would happen should the wind change,

---

¹ *correxit* Wilamowitz : καὶ ἀγαθὰ μετ' Αἰδώς Pap.

i. e. should the Social Revolution ever be achieved. The rich would then be compelled to 'disgorge' (νειόθεν ἐξεμέσαι) all that they possessed.

Compared with this poem and its striking illustration of the social problem in third-century Greece, the second composition contained in Fr. 1 appears less interesting. Cercidas takes as his text the idea expressed in the Tragic fragment

$$\delta\iota\sigma\sigma\grave{a} \ \pi\nu\epsilon\acute{\upsilon}\mu\alpha\tau\alpha \ \pi\nu\epsilon\hat{\iota}\varsigma \ ῎E\rho\omega\varsigma,^{1}$$

which on his evidence we are now able to assign definitely to Euripides. The treatment is once more characteristic of the Cynic method. The text is first paraphrased in a rather burlesque fashion:

Δοιά τις ἁμὶν ἔφα γνάθοισι φυσῆν
τὸν κυανοπτέρυγον παῖδ' Ἀφροδίτας,
Δαμόνομ'· οὔτι γὰρ εἶ λίαν ἀπευθής·
καὶ βροτῶν γὰρ τῷ μὲν ἂν
πραεῖα καὶ εὐμενέουσα²
δεξιτερὰ πνεύσῃ σιαγών,
οὗτος ἐν ἀτρεμίᾳ τὰν ναῦν ἔρωτος
σώφρονι πηδαλίῳ πειθοῦς κυβερνῇ·
τοῖς δὲ τὰν ἀριστερὰν λύσας ἐπόρσῃ
λαίλαπας ἢ λαμυρὰς πόθων ἀέλλας,
κυματίας διόλου τούτοις ὁ πορθμός.
εὖ λέγων Εὐριπίδας.

Then apparently by a gross perversion of Euripides' meaning Cercidas identifies the two kinds of love with those contrasted in Horace's Satire (Sat. i. 2), and in his concluding lines commends, like the Roman poet, the Venus parabilis or, as it is called in the Greek, ἁ ἐξ ἀγορᾶς Ἀφροδίτα. The resemblance between Cercidas's last sentence and lines 125-6 in Horace's satire is very striking, but we can scarcely conclude from this that Horace had read Cercidas.

Fr. 2 appears to contain an attack on luxurious livers who are burdened with useless fat and betrayed by a feverish pulse.³ We may guess that the Cynic ideal of plain living

---

¹ Nauck, Trag. Gr. Frag. Adesp. 187.
² εὐμενέουσα Schmidt, Gött. Gel. Anz., 1912, pp. 634 sqq.: εὐμενε . . . Pap.
³ πιμελὰν μὲν ὠλεσίκαρπον καὶ σφύγα φυσαλέαν. The construction is uncertain.

and self-sufficiency was again inculcated, but the state of the text conceals the details.

Fr. 3 is more autobiographical than the rest. Cercidas addresses his soul, and contrasts his own tranquillity in the face of old age and impending death with the usual reluctance of mankind to close their eyes on this present world. This happy state of mind he attributes to his life-long refusal to yield to the cares which beset the 'sepulchres of fat' (πιμελοσαρκοφάγοι),[1] an attitude which has allowed him to 'pouch' all the 'dainty beasties of the Muses' (ἀβρὰ Μουσᾶν κνώδαλα). Such a strained expression is typical of the Cynics, who aiming at realism constantly fell into similar tastelessness. In the last lines, however, Cercidas seems to express a desire, now that 'his days are looking towards the broad threshold of life's end', for some more serious study than that of poetry, and it is natural to conjecture that, like Virgil in after years, he intended to devote the remainder of his life to philosophy.

Fr. 4, which concludes with the author's subscription mentioned above, and therefore undoubtedly formed the end of the 'book', is too mutilated to give us any certain sense. The mention of ἔρως Ζανωνικός in the last line has been variously interpreted. That Zeno in his 'Republic' had expressed somewhat extreme views on the relations between the sexes is well known; but it is hard to see why some scholars suppose that Cercidas was here controverting those views; for the line taken by Zeno was more Cynic than Stoic, agreeing with the views put forward by Diogenes in his tragedies. On the other hand, later Stoicism tried to explain away or disown its founder's radicalism in these questions.

Similarly in Fr. 5, which according to the convincing suggestion of Mayer[2] is addressed to the Stoic Callimedon, the reference to Sphaerus, the philosophic adviser of Cleomenes, need not be hostile; though if it was written when Sphaerus was actually director of education at Sparta, the assumption would be natural.

---

[1] πιμελοσαρκοφαγῶν Pap., i.e. a participle, certainly wrong: πιμελο-σαρκοφάγων Mayer. Scholars have hitherto taken the word to mean 'eaters of fat flesh'.

[2] *Berl. Phil. Woch.*, 1911, p. 1421.

If we turn now from the matter of Cercidas's poems to their metre and style, we find that the former is much disputed by the scholars who have dealt with the subject. Hunt notes that the metre used in these poems is that commonly known as Dactylo-epitritic, the most favoured combination being the so-called ἐγκωμιολογικὸν Στησιχόρειον (– ‿‿– ‿‿– ᵕ – ‿ – ᵕ), that is to say, the first half of the Hexameter combined with the first half of the Iambus.

Maas,[1] followed by Schmidt and von Arnim, has declared for a much stricter system than that supposed by Hunt. According to him, the poems are really in 'strophes' which correspond with the pauses in the meaning, and the four *cola* which are exclusively employed are combined according to a definite plan. Maas's system works well for some of the fragments, but in others he is compelled to suppose displacement in the text, or, what is worse, a lacuna where the sense is complete. Wilamowitz,[2] who has recently re-examined the whole question, certainly makes a case for much greater variety than is allowed by Maas and von Arnim. The Papyrus leaves the reader to find the colometry, so for the present the question must remain *sub iudice*. It is equally uncertain whether the poems were intended to be read, recited, or sung.

In vocabulary and style Cercidas resembles the writers of the Old Comedy and an author who was slightly his senior, Timon of Phlius. The most noticeable feature is the large number of new words, especially new compounds. The Oxyrhynchus fragments contain some thirty words which were not attested before. Some are easily intelligible, e. g. ἀκρασίων, πενητυλίδας, συοπλουτοσύνα, παραυγῶ (= παραβλέπω), μετεωροκόποι, κυανοπτέρυγος, σκιόθρεπτος, ἀδονόπλακτος (cp. ἡδονοπλήξ in Timon), &c. More strange are ἀποσπαλακῶ, with the meaning 'make blind as a mole' (cp. Hesych. σπαλακία = 'short-sightedness'), Μετάδως, ὀλβοθύλακος λάρος (for ὀλβοθύλακος, which is interpreted in a marginal note as ἀπολαύων, cp. ἀσκοθύλακος in Ar. Fr. 217). Of the

---

[1] *Berl. Phil. Woch.*, 1911, pp. 1011 sqq.
[2] *Sitzungsb. preuss. Akad.*, 1918, pp. 1138 sqq.

τριπλᾶ, or threefold compounds, we have already noticed two : a third occurs in the phrase used in Fr. 1 to describe the poor ἐπιταδεοτρώκτας κοινοκρατηρόσκυφος. There can be no doubt that von Arnim is right in taking this as a collective designation of the needy, whose meals are cut down to what is necessary to avoid starvation, and who, possessing no κρατήρ of their own, are compelled to fill their σκύφος from that which they share with others. Schmidt has pointed out the instructive parallels to Cercidas's formations which are to be found in the Old Comedy, and he is almost certainly correct in asserting that the similarities are to be explained by the fact that both Comedy and Cercidas drew their supply of such words from the vocabulary of the common man. Thus the verbal part in the compounds μετεωροκόπος and ἐπιταδεοτρώκτας seems to be a colloquialism. We find the verb μετεωροκοπεῖν in Ar. Pax 92, and δοξοκόπος, θεατροκόπος, &c., are not uncommon in Hellenistic prose ; while the other compound compared with the Plautine Artotrogus and Miccotrogus shows us that the replacing of ἐσθίω by τρώγω, which is the rule in Modern Greek, and of which we find instances in the New Testament, had already started. Συοπλουτυσύνα finds its nearest parallel in the Aristophanic ὑομουσία (Eq. 986), and the diminutives, δαπάνυλλα (Fr. 1) and ἀπάτυλλα (Fr. 39), are to be compared with the same author's φθίνυλλα (Eccl. 935).

As a Megalopolitan, Cercidas writes in Doric, but how strict his Doric really is, it is difficult to say. The inconsistencies of the papyrus in this matter are exposed by Professor Hunt in his introduction.[1] Like Theocritus, Cercidas permitted himself an epic genitive in οιο (Τυνδαρέοιο, Fr. 1), and alongside of ἐμίν, τίν, λῆς we find forms such as γνάθοισι, φυσιάει, διόλου,[2] &c. It is impossible to say whether his Doric was based on a literary model, or on the spoken language of his time and district, but it is certainly in part artificial. It is possible that he was influenced by Epicharmus, but there is

---

[1] p. 24.
[2] It is suggested that C. picked up διόλου in Athens. It survives in Modern Greek.

nothing remarkable in this.[1] That Cercidas's poems continued to be read long centuries after his death is shown by the references in Galen, Athenaeus, and Gregory; but apart from the passage in Horace already referred to there is little or no trace of later writers having imitated him, unless we follow Susemihl[2] in supposing that the satirist Alcaeus of Messene, who belongs to the next generation, derived some of his verve from the Cynic poet.

E. A. B.

Phoenix.

Phoenix of Colophon, of whom an Ἴαμβος in twenty-two verses is contained in the Heidelberg Papyrus published by Gerhard[3] in 1909, was known to us previously from one reference in Pausanias[4] and five quotations in Athenaeus.[5] The Papyrus in question (P. Heid. 310) contains three poems, viz. one against avarice, one on the right use of wealth, and one against paederasty. The second poem is headed Ἴαμβος Φοίνικος, and this fact alone, apart from considerations of style, is fatal to the view that all three poems are by Phoenix, for in that case we should expect to find the title at the head of the first. We have then an anthology of Choliambic verse (for all three poems are in this metre), which to judge by the script was compiled about the second or third century B. C. Gerhard in his very elaborate commentary tries to establish a Cynic origin for the collection; or perhaps it would be more correct to say that, assuming such an origin, he emends and fills up the text accordingly. Since the first and last poems are anonymous, we can only test his arguments satisfactorily in the case of Phoenix;[6] and here both external and internal

---

[1] Comp. Fr. 2 θεῖ κηλαύνεται, restored by Deubner = Epich. Fr. 216. Fr. 1 σπυροί, a Syracusan form. Fr. 8, Bergk, μαγίς (= τράπεζα), used by Epich. and C. For Fr. 4, Bergk, see above.
[2] *Gesch. d. griech. Litt.* ii, p. 546 n. 140. He compares Alcaeus's οἰνοχάρων, *A. P.* xi. 12. 3, with C.'s λεβητοχάρων, Fr. 6, Bergk.
[3] G. A. Gerhard, *Phoinix von Kolophon*, Leipz. 1909.
[4] Paus. i. 9. 7.
[5] For the fragments preserved by Athenaeus see Gerhard, pp. 179-202.
[6] Comp. P. Vallette, *Rev. de Phil.* xxxvii, pp. 162 sqq.

evidence are against him. Thus Athenaeus always quotes
Phoenix as the 'Iambic poet' only, and the notice in Pausanias is certainly unfavourable to our assigning him to the
Cynic school; for Pausanias tells us that when Lysimachus
destroyed Colophon,[1] Phoenix, a native of the city, lamented
its capture. Such a patriotic tribute would have been
singularly inappropriate in a Cynic, for these philosophers
were particularly proud of their cosmopolitan spirit. Nor, if
we view it impartially, is the internal evidence more favourable to Gerhard. Both the fragments in Athenaeus and the
new Iambus supply us with plenty of moralizing, but there is
nothing distinctively Cynic about it.

The most attractive of the previously known fragments is
the κορώνισμα,[2] in which Phoenix takes as his theme the men
who on certain occasions went round from house to house with
a chough (κορώνη) and sang begging-songs, a custom which
can be paralleled from many ages and countries. The lines
preserved are supposed to be spoken by the strollers at the
house-door. A good idea of the homely character of the
piece is given by lines 8–13 :

> ὦ παῖ, θύρην ἄγκλινε, Πλοῦτος ἔκρουσε,[3]
> καὶ τῇ κορώνῃ παρθένος φέρει σῦκα.
> Θεοί, γένοιτο πάντ' ἄμεμπτος ἡ κούρη,
> κἀφνειὸν ἄνδρα κὠνομαστὸν ἐξεύροι,
> καὶ τῷ γέροντι πατρὶ κοῦρον εἰς χεῖρας
> καὶ μητρὶ κούρην εἰς τὰ γοῦνα κατθείη.

Gerhard compares this house-to-house visit of the κορωνισταί
with the practice of the Cynic philosopher Crates, who from
his habit of entering people's houses to 'labour with' them
was dubbed the ' door-opener' (θυρεπανοίκτης), and classifies
Phoenix's poem as a Cynic begging-song in a folk-lore setting !
But clearly there is nothing to justify this. The moral purpose of Crates, which is made plain in the anecdote of
Diogenes Laertius,[4] has no counterpart in the κορώνισμα ; and

---

[1] The destruction of Colophon is placed between 287 and 281 B.C.
See Gerhard, p. 177.
[2] Fr. 1 Gerhard.   [3] ἔκρουσε Bergk: ἤκουσε Athenaeus.
[4] D. L. vi. 86 ἐκαλεῖτο δὲ καὶ θυρεπανοίκτης διὰ τὸ εἰς πᾶσαν εἰσιέναι οἰκίαν·
καὶ νουθετεῖν.

nothing could be less Cynic than the picture of domestic bliss which is painted in the lines quoted above.

Fr. 2 deals with the epitaph of the Assyrian Ninus, a double of Sardanapalus,[1] who is described as neglecting all his kingly duties, and attending to nothing but eating and drinking. At his death he left inscribed on his tomb a warning against imitation of his own misspent life. This at least seems to be the meaning of the ῥῆσις which Phoenix puts into his mouth. The connexion of this fragment with the many versions of the well-known Sardanapalus epitaph [2] is not quite clear, but even if it is to be considered as a counterblast to the latter, we should remember that the Cynics were not the only persons to protest against the Hedonist theory of life therein inculcated. In the same way it is surely extravagant to connect the blame bestowed on Ninus for not attending to the sacred fire (ll. 5–6) with the fact that a certain sect of the Cynics apparently followed Heraclitus in venerating that element.

The same Ninus is the subject of Fr. 3, where his luxurious life is described in the following figures:

Νίνῳ κάδοι μάχαιρα καὶ κύλιξ αἰχμή,
κύμβη [3] δὲ τόξα, δήιοι δὲ κρητῆρες,
ἵπποι δ᾽ ἄκρητος, κἀλαλὴ " μύρον χεῖτε ".

Fr. 4 is concerned with the famous cup, the prize for wisdom, which made the round of the Seven Sages, a story handled later by Callimachus in his Iambi.[4] The three lines of the Phoenix fragment perhaps suggest that he emphasized the moral worth of Thales. Callimachus, with his usual parade of learning, drags in the Φρὺξ Εὔφορβος, i.e. Pythagoras, and his τρίγωνα σκαληνά.

Fr. 5 is a realistic description of a miser 'pouring with lame fingers bad wine from a broken jar', and reminds us of similar pictures in Horace.

The new Iambus, with its 'diatribe' on wealth, shows us the

---

[1] Comp. D. Serruys, *Rev. de Phil.* xxxvii, pp. 183 sqq.
[2] e.g. *A. P.* vii. 325 :

τόσσ᾽ ἔχω ὅσσ᾽ ἔφαγόν τε καὶ ἔμπιον καὶ μετ᾽ ἐρώτων
τέρπν᾽ ἐδάην· τὰ δὲ πολλὰ καὶ ὄλβια πάντα λέλειπται.

[3] κύμβη Haupt : κόμη Athenaeus.
[4] Fr. 83 a, 89, 94–6, Schneider, and Oxyrhynchus Papyri, vii, pp. 31-3.

same man, though certainly the tone is more vigorous, and at least one phrase, if Crusius's suggestion is correct, exhibits the Cynic's brutality. The first twelve lines are tolerably well preserved :

Πολλοῖς γε θνητῶν τἀγάθ᾽, ὦ Ποσείδιππε,[1]
οὐ σύμφορ᾽ ἐστίν, ἀλλ᾽ ἔδει[2] τοιαῦτ᾽ αὐτοὺς
πλουτεῖν[3] ὁκοῖα καὶ φρονεῖν ἐπίστανται·
νῦν δ᾽ οἱ μὲν ἡμῶν[4] κρήγυοι καθεστῶτες
πολλὴν ἀφειδέως νηστείην[5] ἐρεύγονται,
οἱ δ᾽ οὔτε σῦκα, φασίν, οὔτ᾽ ἐρῖν᾽ εὔντες
πλουτοῦσι, τῷ πλούτῳ δὲ πρὸς τί δεῖ χρῆσθαι,
τοῦτ᾽ αὐτὸ πάντων πρῶτον οὐκ ἐπίστανται,
ἀλλ᾽ οἰκίας μὲν ἐκ λίθου σμαραγδίτου
εἴ πως ἀνυστόν ἐστι τοῦτ᾽ αὐτοῖς πρήσσειν,
αὐλάς[6] τ᾽ ἐχούσας καὶ στοὰς τετραστύλους
πολλῶν ταλάντων ἀξίας κατακτῶνται . . .

The lines which follow are too mutilated to give a certain sense, but it is obvious that the poet contrasted the moral and intellectual poverty of these millionaires with their material prosperity. The conclusion emerges more clearly :

Τοῖς οὖν τοιούτοις ἀνδράσιν, Ποσείδιππε,
οὐ συμβέβηκεν οἰκίας μὲν κεκτῆσθαι
καλὰς καταξίας τε χρημάτων πολλῶν,
αὐτοὺς δ᾽ ὑπάρχειν ἀξίους τριῶν χαλκῶν;

We note that like other moralists Phoenix, despite his contempt for the rich, seems not wholly untouched by envy of them. If there is nothing remarkable about the homely moralizing of this writer, neither does the form of his compositions show us anything out of the way. Unlike Cercidas, he has no strange compounds: his vocabulary is that of everyday life. The only author whom he appears to imitate is Hipponax, the originator in the sixth century of the Greek Choliambic. In the early Hellenistic age, for reasons which are not quite obvious but are probably connected with the

---

[1] Probably Poseidippus the Epigrammatist. Comp. Gerhard, pp. 103-4.
[2] ἔδει Bucherer: ἀλλὰ δεῖ Pap.   [3] πλουτεῖν Sitzler.
[4] νῦν δ᾽ οἱ μὲν ἡμῶν Crusius.
[5] νηστείην Crusius. For quantity of ει comp. Nairn, *Herodas*, Introd., p. lxxxii.
[6] αὐλάς *supplevit* Sitzler.

revival of Ionic culture after the period of Athenian predomi-
nance, Hipponax enjoyed a considerable vogue not only
among the Alexandrians proper, e. g. Callimachus and Herondas, but also and less surprisingly among the Cynics and
other popular moralists. The plebeian satirist of Ephesus
formed an admirable model for these 'barking' missionaries,
and in their hands the old Ionian Iambus, revived after three
centuries, took a form which undoubtedly influenced later
satire, both Greek and Roman. In Phoenix we find traces of
Hipponax's influence in the vocabulary,[1] and once at least in
the phrasing.[2]

The dialect of these pieces is Ionic, but Attic forms taken
from the Κοινή of the day are not infrequent. Some of these
are perhaps to be explained, as Hense[3] thinks, by a fondness
for alliteration, the letter π being especially favoured for this
purpose. In his handling of the Choliambic metre Phoenix,
like the authors of the other fragments published by Gerhard,
does not appear to be conscious of the convention, first
observable in Herondas and invariable in Babrius, according
to which the penultimate syllable in each line always has an
accent on it. This is what we should expect from one whose
floruit is to be placed at the beginning of the Alexandrian
epoch, and who was unaffected by the refinements of later
versifiers. It also affords some evidence that the authors of
the anonymous pieces were more or less contemporary with
Phoenix.

Anonymous Fragments in the Heidelberg Papyrus.

The two anonymous poems in P. Heid. 310 need not detain
us long. The first piece, of which about forty lines are
preserved in a more or less intelligible condition, attacks the
vice of αἰσχροκέρδεια, a vice condemned by Greek public
opinion no less than by the teaching of the Cynics. On the

---

[1] λέκος πυρῶν Fr. 1, l. 2 = Hippon. Fr. 58. Κόραξος Fr. 2, l. 14 =
Hippon. Fr. 3. Σινδός Fr. 2, l. 15 = Hippon. Fr. 68 A.
[2] οὐ γὰρ ἀλλὰ κηρύσσω Fr. 2, l. 15 = Hippon. Fr. 13.
[3] *Berl. Phil. Woch.*, 1910, pp. 1061 sqq.

other hand, a definitely non-Cynic feature is the emphasis laid on the offence against religion which such a vice constitutes (ll. 37-8). The author apparently believes in the power of Heaven to bring about some sort of retribution even in this life :

Ἔστιν γάρ, ἔστιν, ὃς τάδε σκοπεῖ δαίμων,
ὃς ἐν χρόνῳ τὸ θεῖον οὐ καταισχύνει,
νέμει δ᾽ ἑκάστῳ τὴν καταισίαν μοῖραν.[1]

The style is just as simple and popular as that of Phoenix, and the language even closer to that of the Κοινή.

We can safely conjecture from the *disiecta membra* which survive of the third poem in the collection that it dealt with the subject mentioned above, but as no single line has been preserved entire it is hazardous to determine how that subject was treated.

Anonymous Fragments in the London and Bodleian Papyri.

Along with the Heidelberg Papyrus, Gerhard published two other fragments of Choliambic verse. The first of these, which is labelled P. Lond. 155, contains forty-one lines, of which about ten are tolerably well preserved. The writing according to Kenyon is perhaps to be assigned to the third century A. D. The second fragment (P. Bodl. MS. Gr. class f, 1 (p)) is considerably older, belonging probably to the second century B. C. From the remnants of thirteen lines which it contains we see that the poem is identical with that in the London fragment. The two fragments therefore can be used to supplement each other in the reconstruction of the text. Even then we do not obtain much for our pains. Once more it is the selfish money-grubbing tendency of the age which is censured. The points made are those so familiar in all similar literature, e. g. ' Every one is the rich man's friend, the poor man is loathed even by his family ', or as the author puts it (ll. 23-5) :

ἐπὴν ἔχῃς τι, πάντα σοι φίλων πλήρη·
πλουτοῦντα γάρ σε χοἰ θεοὶ φιλήσουσι,
πένητα δ᾽ ὄντα χἠ τεκοῦσα μεισήσει.

---

[1] ll. 67-9.

He himself is apparently one of these unfortunate poor, but he refuses to bow down to his contemptuous superiors:

πάντας ἀνθρώπους μεισῶ
τοὺς ζῶντας οὕτω, κἄτι μᾶλλον μεισήσω. (ll. 28–9.)

In connexion with these lines it is worth noting that the 'misanthrope' type was apparently first developed in the literature of the early Hellenistic age.[1]

E. A. B.

Chares.

Chares,[2] of whom a fragmentary extract of some fifty-five lines has come to light in a Papyrus of the first part of the third century B. C., is little more than a name. Three fragments preserved by Stobaeus are given by Nauck, *T. F.*, p. 826. He wrote Γνῶμαι, prudential maxims, and six of the newly-discovered lines already appear in the collection of Γνῶμαι μονόστιχοι appended to the fragments of Menander. Although Chares' name does not appear in the new fragments, their authorship is unquestionable, since two of the lines are fortunately found in Stobaeus with Chares' name prefixed. The general tone of the lines is very like that of the treatise 'Ad Demonicum', which we need not refuse, as some critics have done, to attribute to Isocrates. They may be compared with an Inscription containing a large number of brief aphorisms, of the date of about 300 B. C., found in the neighbourhood of Cyzicus.[3]

Pseud-Epicharmea.

Athenaeus,[4] when speaking of 'those who composed (πεποιηκότες) the poems attributed to Epicharmus', says that, according to Aristoxenus, the flute-player Chrysogonus, who lived at the end of the fifth century, was the author of τὰ ψευδεπιχάρμεια ταῦτα; and that, according to Philochorus, the author of the Ἀτθίς, and to Apollodorus, the Κανών and the Γνῶμαι were the work of Axiopistus, who is thought to have lived in the fourth century. But how much he edited, and

---

[1] Comp. Gerhard, pp. 170 sqq.
[2] Χάρητος Γνῶμαι. G. A. Gerhard, *Sitzungsb. d. Heidelberger Akademie*, 1912.
[3] Hasluck in *Journal of Hellenic Studies*, vol. xxvii, pp. 61, 62.
[4] Athen. xiv. 648 D.

how much he composed, is uncertain, just as we cannot determine how much of 'Theognis' is the author's, and how much is accretion.

Sententious quotations from 'Epicharmus' appear as early as Xenophon[1] and Plato[2] and in Aristotle's *Rhetoric*;[3] but it it is better to call them 'quotations of an Epicharmean character', rather than 'quotations from Epicharmus'.

The following are the fragments, all in Trochaic Tetrameters, but not in the strict Doric of Epicharmus himself:

(1) Some thirty lines in *Hibeh Papyri*, i. 1,[4] a papyrus of the date 220 to 240 B.C.

(2) A few more fragmentary lines in *Hibeh Papyri*, i. 2, of the same date.

(3) Two fragments in the Berlin *Klass. Texte*, V. ii. 124, from a papyrus of the second century B.C.

(4) Two fragments on a potsherd of the third century A.D. (*Sitzungsb. d. preuss. Akad.*, 1918, p. 742).

It might be observed that the fragment of ten lines with Scholia in Kaibel, *Com. Gr. Frag.*, No. 99, from a Papyrus, is genuine Epicharmus, belonging to the Ὀδυσσεὺς Αὐτόμολος. This is another indication that the other fragments are not by Epicharmus, since they have no Scholia; whereas these plainly come from a learned edition of the works of the poet brought out at Alexandria.

The first in the preceding list is obviously a proem to a handbook of maxims for conduct in all departments of life:

Τεῖδ' ἔνεστι πολλὰ καὶ παντοῖα, τοῖς χρήσαιό κα
ποτὶ φίλον, ποτ' ἐχθρόν, ἐν δίκᾳ λέγων, ἐν ἁλίᾳ,
ποτὶ πονηρόν, ποτὶ καλόν τε κἀγαθόν, ποτὶ ξένον,
ποτὶ δύσηριν, ποτὶ πάροινον, ποτὶ βάναυσον, αἴτε τις
ἀλλ' ἔχει κακόν τι, καὶ τούτοισι κέντρ' ἔνο.
Ἐν δὲ καὶ γνῶμαι σοφαὶ τεῖδ', αἷσιν εἰ πίθοιτό τις,
δεξιώτερός τέ κ' εἴη βελτίων τ' ἐς πάντ' ἀνήρ.

Now it so happens that a number of single lines are quoted by Plutarch, Stobaeus, Clement of Alexandria, and others,

[1] Two in Xen. *Memor.* ii. 1. 20.
[2] A paraphrase; Plato, *Gorg.* 508 E.
[3] Arist. *Rhet.* ii. 21. 6.
[4] *Hibeh Papyri*, i, Grenfell and Hunt.

giving such maxims; and it is an attractive conjecture of Crönert[1] that these are taken from the work of which we have here a fragment, and that the fragment is actually the Preface to them. And he finds one existing fragment of five lines from Diogenes Laertius,[2] which would do very well for the conclusion of the Preface.

The second set of fragments, also in Trochaic Tetrameters, appears to belong to another work of the nature of proverbial philosophy. The papyrus is of the same date as the first, but the two are not parts of the same manuscript. In one of the fragments where the beginnings of the lines are preserved, the single lines are marked off by Paragraphi into μονόστιχοι; and the facts that Chares wrote in this style, and in Trochaic Tetrameters, and that both this Papyrus and that containing the fragments of Chares probably came from mummy-wrappings in the same locality, Hibeh, make it quite possible that we have here more fragments of Chares.

The third set are from a papyrus of the second century B.C.; the first is on the fierce temper of women ' who bite the hand that feeds them ' (a certain restoration); the second is on the theme that ' marriage is a lottery '. The lines are forcible and concise :

> τὸ δὲ γαμεῖν ὅμοιόν ἐστι τῷ τρὶς ἓξ ἢ τρεῖς μόνους
> ἀπὸ τύχης βαλεῖν· ἐὰν μὲν γὰρ λάβῃς τεταγμέναν
> τοῖς τρόποις καὶ τἄλλ' ἄλυπον, εὐτυχήσεις τῷ γάμῳ·
> εἰ δέ κα φιλόξενόν τε καὶ λάλον καὶ δαψιλῆ,
> οὐ γυναῖχ' ἕξεις, διὰ βίου δ' ἀτυχίαν κοσμουμέναν.

The fourth set consists of three lines on ' the fool ' :

> . . χῶρος οἰκία τυραννὶς πλοῦτος ἰσχὺς καλλονὰ
> ἄφρονος ἀνθρώπου τυχόντα καταγέλαστα γίνεται,

a sentiment expressed in language closely resembling a fragment of Aristotle [3] which we possess ; and two lines comparing wicked pleasures to pirates :

> ἀδοναὶ δ' εἰσὶν βροτοῖσιν ἀνόσιοι λᾳστήριοι,
> καταπεπόντισται γὰρ εὐθὺς ἀδοναῖς ἀνὴρ ἀλούς.

[1] *Hermes*, xlvii. 402.
[2] Epicharmus, Kaibel, *Com. Graec. Frag.* 254, from Diog. Laert. iii. 12.17.
[3] Arist. Fr. 57, Rose³, ap. Stob. iii, p. 200, Wach.-H.

Both these fragments show the same forcibleness and conciseness as the third set.

J. U. P.

Philodemus.

'The unrolling and deciphering of the Herculaneum Papyri', writes Sudhaus,[1] 'was approached with intense excitement. What might not these rolls contain, survivors, as by a miracle, of 2,000 years, almost " despite the stars and fate " ? Madame de Staël " trembles to breathe, from fear lest a breath should blow away this dust, in which perhaps noble thoughts still slumber ".

'The spell begins to break. Hands are laid on the ancient treasure. Well-known authors turn up—Epicurus, Metrodorus, Hermarchus, Colotes, Polystratus, once even an isolated Stoic, Chrysippus. But again and again in the collection appears the name of Philodemus, sometimes with several copies of one work , . .

'What a disappointment! and who will sort these shreds? Who will fill out the gaping, monstrous, gaps? Who indeed will even read the black-brown text? For here one's eye glides over no smooth paper surface, but must often dive into deep folds and cracks, to see if this stroke expands into A or M. And if, baked by Naples' sun, one breathes too deep, the fear of Madame de Staël becomes tragic truth, and A or M flutters off. Perhaps it was A after all. What a disappointment ! '

Philodemus was in fact almost unknown before these Papyri were unrolled. Half a dozen references in Cicero, Strabo, and Diogenes Laertius informed us that there was an Epicurean of that name, from Gadara in Syria, a pupil of Zeno of Sidon, who presided over the school of Epicurus at Athens round about 100 B.C. Certain Epigrams of his were preserved in the Anthology, and we had the evidence of Cicero, an acquaintance and contemporary, for the fact that he was both a pleasant

---

[1] *Philodemi Volumina Rhetorica: Supplementum* (Teubner, 1895). The death of this brilliant scholar in action during the war is a serious loss to learning. He had in hand further important work on Epicurean material, as well as on the new Menander.

and a learned person [1] (coupled in this verdict with another Epicurean, Siron, the reputed teacher of Virgil). Apart from these Epigrams not a word of his writing survived.

It is probable that the library disinterred at Herculaneum was previously Philodemus's own. This would account for the large number of works by him as well as for its almost purely Epicurean character. Evidently the Gulf of Naples was the centre of Italian Epicureanism, and the numerous works of Philodemus were written for and circulated among the members of that community.[2] This community is perhaps the 'associates of Philodemus' referred to by Diogenes Laertius (x. 24). Philodemus does not pretend to be an original philosopher. Of course, in a sense, no Epicurean pretended to be that. Their fidelity to their master and to his immediate associates was a byword, a cause at once of the ridicule and of the envy of rival schools. Epicurus was a Saviour, and his words were verbally inspired. The controversies within the school recorded by Philodemus were controversies as to what Epicurus or Metrodorus, or one of the other masters, really said or meant. It is on these terms that the Epicureans of Rhodes, Rome, Cos, and Athens fall out (*Rhet.* i. 89 ; *Suppl.* 44), messengers going to and fro between Athens and the provinces to get and give the official interpretation. Philodemus complains that disputants often do not even take the trouble to check their references. They say, 'Epicurus wrote thus', and they cannot say where. Sometimes, too, they misquote. It is on similar terms that Philodemus disputes with 'dearest Bromios', his fellow-pupil. The nearest parallel at the present day to the tone and method of these disputes is to be found in the controversies between the followers of the Socialist prophet, Karl Marx. The recent dispute between Lenin and Karl Kautsky as to the nature of the 'Dictatorship of the Proletariat' is not primarily a dispute as to what is right or just or good, but as

[1] But Cicero (*in Pisonem*, xxviii, xxix) also regards him as having had a bad influence upon Piso, which to judge from the tone of some of the Epigrams, is not unlikely. The speech, however, is an attack on Philodemus's patron, Piso, and Cicero would not disdain to take advantage in the law courts of the popular prejudice against Epicureans as immoral people.

[2] Pap. 312 (Crönert, *Kolotes u. Menedemos*, pp. 125–7, 132).

to the precise meaning to be attached to certain phrases used by Marx and Engels.

But the unoriginality of Philodemus goes farther than this. As a good Epicurean he accepts the dogma of the verbal inspiration of the master, with the corollary that any speculation in which the school may indulge is of the nature of interpretation or exegesis. Even the interpretation, however, which he expounds is not his own. It is apparently throughout that of the man who was head of the school when he was a student at Athens, Zeno of Sidon. This is not only definitely established in regard to many books and passages in which Zeno is referred to by name as source,[1] but also generally by the fact that the controversies between the various philosophical schools to which Philodemus introduces us are almost exclusively those of the second century B. C., not of the first. Perhaps the most influential philosophical writer contemporary with Philodemus was the Stoic Posidonius. Posidonius's influence upon Cicero is unquestioned. In Philodemus, however, there is only one known reference to Posidonius (in an unpublished Papyrus), and, in spite of innumerable references to the Stoics, there is hardly a trace of doctrine which might be supposed to be his. The explanation is obvious. Posidonius was some thirty years younger than Zeno, and the polemics of Philodemus are those of Zeno's lectures.[2] Philodemus in fact was a popular writer of philosophy, and the philosophy which he popularized was substantially that which he had learned as a student at Athens years before.

No doubt philosophy which is derivative to this extent has little intrinsic value. But ancient writers ' took what they required ' so frankly and simply, keeping close to the wording

---

[1] For the evidence as to the relation of Philodemus to Zeno, see Crönert, *Kol. u. Men.*, pp. 175-6; Susemihl, *Griech. Lit. in d. Alexandrinerzeit*, vol. ii, pp. 264, 267 ff. Three titles explicitly admit derivation from Zeno (ἐκ τῶν Ζήνωνος σχολῶν—the last word not quite certain).

[2] Diels, *Phil. über die Götter: Erstes Buch*, p. 53; Crönert, *Kol. u. Men.*, pp. 24, 133, 177. Posidonius would be some twenty years older than Philodemus. Zeno's teaching activity was from 120 to 78 B.C. The chief representative of the Stoics to Philodemus is Diogenes Babylonius; of the Peripatetics, Critolaus. Both belong to the middle of the second century. On the question of the gods, however, Crönert assumes a controversy between Zeno and Posidonius, op. cit., n. 512, p. 113.

of their originals, even when not actually quoting—and Philodemus is full of verbal citations, many of which cannot yet with certainty be assigned to an author—that, in the absence of the originals, compilations of this kind may acquire first-rate importance. It must be remembered that the work of deciphering and interpreting the Papyri is so difficult and laborious, that progress can only be very slow. Philodemus is therefore still to some extent hidden treasure, from which far greater returns are likely in the future than any as yet realized. But even so, the acute and exemplary work of modern German scholars, particularly of Gomperz, Sudhaus, and Crönert, has succeeded in extracting from the Papyri a mass of material which is of quite cardinal importance for the history of Greek philosophy between the fourth and first centuries B. C.

This material is of service in three main directions. (1) We have, in the first place, in Philodemus a first-rate source of information as to Epicurean doctrine and terminology. The logical tract περὶ σημείων καὶ σημειώσεων, which expounds Zeno's teaching in regard to what we now call inductive argument, fills what was previously an absolute gap in our knowledge of the Epicurean school. Its intrinsic value has been differently estimated by different writers. The adverse verdict of Zeller [1] is certainly over-severe. Mill's celebrated question (which baffled 'the wisest of the ancients') states precisely the problem which Zeno tried to face. ' Why is a single instance, in some cases, sufficient for a complete induction, while in others, myriads of concurring instances, without a single exception known or presumed, go such a very little way towards establishing a universal proposition?' A Greek attempt to answer this question can hardly fail to be interesting, even though hampered, as Zeller complains, by Epicurean sensationalism and by the lack of a conception of the Uniformity of Nature. And in another respect this tract has a peculiar interest. It is the only attempt, as far as we know, by the followers of Epicurus to break new ground beyond the lines laid down by the founders of the school. No other tract has quite this unique character. For the most part the others

[1] *Phil. d. Gr.*⁴ iii, pp. 405 ff.

tread familiar ground, and merely fill out with additional detail doctrines already familiar from other sources. But the detail is of immense value for the interpretation of other surviving documents of the school ; in particular, of the letters of Epicurus and the poem of Lucretius. True to the atmosphere of the time and to the tradition of the school, Philodemus has one constant peroration, the praise of the philosophic life. To this theme, with its infinite variations, all inquiries lead.

(2) In the second place Philodemus's writings contain a mass of evidence as to the activities and personalities of other philosophical schools, particularly, as has already been remarked, during the second century. Some of the evidence lies on the face of these writings, where the text is reasonably well-preserved and where the rival thinker is in the main current of the argument. It is Philodemus's way to state very fully the views impugned. His methods can be well seen in the tract *On Economy* (the ninth book of a comprehensive work *On the Vices and their Opposed Virtues*), directed against two works still extant, the *Oeconomicus* of Xenophon and the *Oeconomica* of Aristotle. (There has always been some doubt as to the authorship of the last-named work, and it is interesting that Philodemus refers to it as a work of Theophrastus.) We find that Philodemus keeps very close to the wording of the original. We can therefore expect with increasing knowledge of the Herculaneum Papyri to extend considerably our knowledge of Diogenes Babylonius, Critolaus, and other lesser lights of the Stoic and Peripatetic schools. There are also cursory references to other schools of philosophy as well as to philosophers whose school is unknown. Many of the latter are no doubt minor Epicureans. These references open a wide field for ingenious and hazardous conjecture, of which Crönert's *Kolotes und Menedemos* gives many brilliant specimens. In particular, the rhetorical works add considerably to our knowledge of the controversies concerning the proper place and function of rhetoric, one of the burning questions of the time.[1] Lastly, special mention should be made of the very interesting

---

[1] See Sudhaus, *Voll. Rhet.*, preface to vol. i and (especially) to the *Supplementum.*

summary of a letter of Aristo of Ceos contained in the tenth book of the work *On the Vices*. Aristo of Ceos was a Peripatetic of the third century,[1] who analysed the weakness of human nature in the Theophrastean manner. Two-thirds of the forty-three pages of text printed by Jensen is professedly a summary of a letter written by Aristo on the subject how one may best rid oneself of the insolence of pride (περὶ τοῦ κουφίζειν ὑπερηφανίας).

(3) Thirdly, as a result of all this information as to the writers of this period and their works, Philodemus throws considerable light on the vexed and tangled problems concerning the sources of the later philosophical writers. Comparison of his text with Cicero, Plutarch, Seneca, and other writers, gives many valuable hints in a field in which a hint is usually as much as can be expected ; and the problem of problems, that of the sources of Diogenes Laertius, has been considerably advanced as a result of the study of the Herculaneum Papyri.

Even after making every allowance for the shocking state of most of the text and for the conjectural character of its restoration, it must be admitted that Philodemus does not write very easy or attractive Greek. He is evidently a writer of some literary pretensions. For instance, he uniformly avoids hiatus. But his sentences are long and involved, not occasionally and for the sake of an effect, but with a tedious and uniform monotony. In the *Supplementum* to his edition of the rhetorical writings Sudhaus has set out most of Book I and II of the *De Rhetorica* (it is not really a ' Rhetoric ' but a discussion of the nature and place of rhetoric in life) as a continuous piece of prose, liberating Philodemus from the tyranny of its papyrus-versicles, under which otherwise the unfortunate author everywhere suffers, bonds particularly galling to an author who loves long sentences. How would his friend Cicero read, printed in such a guise ? This little Teubner text of sixty-two pages gives the best idea, to any one who is not expert in dealing with printed Papyri, of the style and manner of Philodemus. The result is on the whole reassuring, and makes one at least

---

[1] Not to be confused with the Stoic of that name, who came from Chios and flourished about the same time.

suspect that Philodemus's style has been over-abused. The fifth book of the *De Rhetorica* (Sudhaus, vol. ii, pp. 131–67, and vol. i, pp. 231–70)—a comparison of the merits of philosophy and rhetoric, which is fairly well preserved—also seems to justify a not unfavourable verdict on Philodemus's literary powers, though the faults of repetition and verbosity must be conceded.

The date of Philodemus's writings cannot be determined with certainty. The περὶ σημείων mentions [1] some dwarfs brought recently (νῦν) by Antony from Syria. This must refer to the Syrian expedition of the Proconsul Gabinius; and 54 B. C. is fixed as the earliest date for the composition of that book.[2] There is also an apparent reference in an unpublished papyrus to Cicero's proconsulate in Cilicia (51–50 B. C.).[3] Antony occurs again in the first book of the work *On the Gods* in a context which suggests the year 44 B. C.[3]

We know from Diogenes Laertius (x. 3) that Philodemus wrote a work in at least ten books (he quotes from the tenth) entitled ἡ τῶν φιλοσόφων σύνταξις, no doubt a comprehensive survey of the schools of philosophy, detailing the leading members of each in chronological order. No roll bearing this title has survived, but the list of Academic philosophers, which has been edited by Mekler, is usually supposed to be a part of this work. Fragments have also been deciphered of a similar list of the Stoics, and of some of the Pre-Socratics.[4] This is the only work of Philodemus of which we have evidence independent of Herculaneum.

Considerable fragments survive of another comprehensive compilation, which bears the title περὶ τῶν κακιῶν καὶ τῶν ἀντικειμένων ἀρετῶν. Of this work Books IX and X have been separately edited ; but apparently there is a good deal more, particularly a long discussion of κολακεία in more than one book, which is fairly well preserved. Further, the περὶ παρρησίας probably belongs to this work. In its title it is said

[1] Ed. Gomperz, p. 4 (col. 2).
[2] Philippson, *De Philodemi libro* π. σημ., p. 6 ; Diels, *Phil. über die Götter: Erstes Buch*, p. 99.   [3] Diels, l. c.
[4] Crönert, *Kol. u. Men.*, pp. 130–3, gives a survey of the rolls which may be supposed to belong to this work, and also prints some portions of the surviving fragments.

to be a part of the περὶ ἠθῶν καὶ βίων : but this is generally supposed to have been an alternative title of the περὶ κακιῶν. Perhaps it was the title of the lectures of Zeno on which the work was based.

Other works in more than two books are the following : περὶ θεῶν, περὶ θανάτου, both dealing with current superstitions, freedom from which was one of the main objectives of Epicurean effort ; περὶ ῥητορικῆς, περὶ μουσικῆς, περὶ ποιημάτων, discussing the value of these arts for human life. Besides these, there are numerous shorter works, of some of which the title only is known, while of others the title is lost. They are of very various character, but predominantly ethical, if one may include under this name discussions concerning the gods and on such subjects as the value of rhetoric. There are no physical tracts, but the library contained Epicurus's great work, the περὶ φύσεως, in thirty-seven books. Fragments of many books of this work have survived, and reconstructions of many of the best-preserved fragments have been published in various periodicals.[1] Orelli's inadequate treatment of the fragments of Books II and XI (Leipzig, 1818) is the nearest approach to an edition. A complete edition of the surviving fragments has long been promised, and is urgently needed. There are some other logical tracts besides the περὶ σημείων. In addition there are biographical tracts, a discourse on Epicurus, on the Stoics, and other contributions to the history of philosophy. In all, traces of about thirty works by Philodemus have survived, a considerable testimony to industry at a time when writing books was more difficult than it is now.

It is beyond the scope of this sketch to attempt a complete list of the many books and periodicals in which surviving fragments of these rolls may be found. But most of the best-preserved rolls have now been issued separately. The following is a list of the most recent editions of each of these, arranged in alphabetical order of editors.

Περὶ θεῶν, lib. i, iii : ed. H. Diels (*Abh. der Kgl. Preuss. Akad. d. Wiss., philos.-hist. Kl.*, 1915 and 1917). Published separately, 1916, 1917.

[1] See note on p. 40.

PHILODEMUS 29

Περὶ σημείων καὶ σημειώσεων : ed. T. Gomperz (*Herkulanische Studien*, i. Heft). 1865. Teubner.
Περὶ εὐσεβείας : ed. T. Gomperz (*Herk. St.*, ii. Heft). 1866. Teubner.[1]
Περὶ ποιημάτων, lib. ii : ed. A. Hausrath (*Jahrbuch f. klass. Philologic, Supplementum*). 1889. Teubner.
Περὶ οἰκονομίας [= περὶ κακιῶν, lib. ix] : ed. C. Jensen. 1906. Teubner.[2]
Περὶ κακιῶν, lib. x : ed. C. Jensen. 1911. Teubner.[2]
Περὶ μουσικῆς : ed. I. Kemke. 1884. Teubner.[2]
Περὶ θανάτου, lib. iv : ed. S. Mekler (*Sitzb. der Wiener Akad., philos.-hist. Kl.*). 1886.
Περὶ τοῦ καθ᾽ Ὅμηρον ἀγαθοῦ βασιλέως : ed. A. Olivi i. 1909. Teubner.[2]
Περὶ παρρησίας [a section of a larger work, based on Zeno, περὶ ἠθῶν καὶ βίων[3]] : ed. A. Olivieri. 1914. Teubner.[2]
Volumina Rhetorica [περὶ ῥητορικῆς and περὶ ῥητορικῆς ὑπομνηματικόν] : ed. S. Sudhaus. Vol. i, 1892. Vol. ii, 1896. *Supplementum*, 1895. Teubner.[2]
Περὶ ὀργῆς : ed. C. Wilke. 1914. Teubner.[2]

To these should be added the following, not published under Philodemus's name :

Fragmenta Herculanensia, by W. Scott. 1884. Oxford. [Contains fragments of several works other than those mentioned above.]

Academicorum Philosophorum Index Herculanensis : ed. S. Mekler. 1902. Weidmann. [Probably a section of the φιλοσόφων σύνταξις.]

Herculanensium Voluminum Quae Supersunt : Collectio Tertia : ed. D. Bassi. 1914. Milan. [Contains περὶ θανάτου, lib. iv, and a book of the περὶ κακιῶν (Pap. 1457).]

[A full list of the literature will be found in Ueberweg's *Grundriss d. Geschichte d. Philosophie* (ed. K. Praechter, 1920), pp. 463-6.]

J. L. S.

Polystratus.

Polystratus is given by Diogenes Laertius as the third head of the Epicurean school, following Hermarchus, who was the immediate successor of Epicurus.[4] The date of his accession is not known ; but Epicurus died in 271/0. He belongs therefore to the middle of the third century, and may have heard Epicurus himself. But the lack of reference to Polystratus

[1] A great deal of new work has been published on this book since 1866. Philippson's article in *Hermes*, lv (July 1920), is the first instalment of what is practically a new edition of the text, drastically rearranging the fragments.
[2] In the ordinary Teubner series of Greek texts.
[3] Probably an alternative title for the περὶ κακιῶν.
[4] There is also a story preserved by Valerius Maximus that he shared the command of the school with his inseparable friend Hippoclides—'eodem die nati . . . eodemque momento temporis ultima senectute exstincti.' Usener, *Epicurea* : Index Nominum, s. v. Ἱπποκλείδης.

in the writings of Philodemus shows that he had not the same position in the school as Hermarchus, Metrodorus, and Polyaenus, the immediate associates of Epicurus referred to by Philodemus as 'the masters' (καθηγεμόνες).

There are two works among the Herculaneum Papyri which bear the name of Polystratus. Of one, entitled περὶ φιλοσοφίας (both Metrodorus and Polyaenus, it seems, also wrote works under this title), only broken fragments can be deciphered.[1] The other is better preserved. It has the title περὶ ἀλόγου καταφρονήσεως, with the alternative πρὸς τοὺς ἀλόγως καταθρασυνομένους τῶν ἐν τοῖς πολλοῖς δοξαζομένων, and is published separately in a slim volume, edited by C. Wilke, in the Teubner series. The unjustified 'contempt' or 'self-confidence' is that of rival schools of philosophy, which is contrasted with the well-justified confidence of the Epicurean, and his firmly grounded contempt for the fears and superstitions of the vulgar and the delusions of other schools of thought. The special complaint against the schools criticized seems to be that their conclusions are such as could not be practised without disaster, and hence that they do not practise what they preach.[2] There is some doubt as to who Polystratus's adversaries were. The suggestion that they were Stoic has little plausibility. The Cynic school is actually mentioned; and the thesis that good and bad is a merely conventional distinction, to the discussion of which a third of the surviving text is devoted, is attributed by Sextus Empiricus, as Wilke points out, to the Sceptics. For this and other reasons Wilke thinks that the main adversaries were the followers of Pyrrho. However this may be, the argument for the objectivity of good and evil is the really valuable part of the book. Polystratus develops arguments not familiar from other Epicurean sources, which we should be glad to have at greater length. The recurring theme of the whole work is, inevitably, praise of the Epicurean philosophic method, as the only road to delivery from fear and superstition. This alone guarantees the 'free life'—μόνη τὸν ἐλεύθερον βίον παρασκευάζει.   J. L. S.

[1] See Crönert, *Kol. u. Men.*, pp. 35-6.
[2] The topic of the relation of philosophic opinion to the vulgar is dealt with in a somewhat similar way in the *Rhetoric* of Philodemus (S., vol. i, pp. 253 ff.).

APPENDIX

The Later Epicureanism : Diogenes of Oenoanda.

The account of newly-discovered Greek Moralists would be incomplete without the names of Diogenes of Oenoanda and Hierocles, although they fall outside the limits of our period. A novel and fascinating monument of ancient philosophy was discovered in 1884 by the French scholars, Holleaux and Paris, who first hit upon the remains of the elaborate Lycian Inscription which we now know as the fragments of Diogenes of Oenoanda. There was considerable difficulty in sorting the stones ; in determining their sequence, and in filling the many lacunae satisfactorily. But the labours of a succession of scholars have gone far to solve these problems; and now in the excellent edition of Johann William,[1] with its illuminating introduction and notes, the fragments are accessible to students of classical literature in an intelligible order and form, which, though no doubt not final, is yet not likely to be substantially altered as the result of further inquiries and consideration.

Epigraphical and linguistic considerations combine to warrant the view that the inscription belongs to the latter part of the second century of the Christian era.[2] There is no other internal evidence as to its date, and external evidence is altogether lacking. The motive and character of the inscription is fully explained in the remaining fragments. Diogenes is a man saved by the Epicurean faith, and he wishes to share the means of salvation with his fellow citizens. And not only with them. He hopes that future generations also will have cause to bless his name, and no less the strangers or foreigners,

[1] *Diogenis Oenoandensis Fragmenta* : ordinavit et explicavit Iohannes William. Leipzig, 1907. (Bibl. Scr. Gr. et Rom. Teubneriana.) *Bulletin de Corr. Hellénique*, vols. xvi and xxi.

[2] Oenoanda was in the Roman province of Lycia, situated about thirty miles inland from the western coast opposite Rhodes. In view of the distinguished philosophical history of the island, it is worth noticing that the fragments warrant the view that Rhodes was to Diogenes the philosophical centre of the district. We know from Philodemus that there was an Epicurean circle at Rhodes in the first century, which was in close touch with Athens ; we also know from other sources that the Peripatetic philosophy continued to flourish there for several centuries. It is interesting to discover that the Epicurean school was still active in the island two centuries after Philodemus wrote.

wrongly so called (τοὺς καλουμένους μὲν ξένους, οὐ μήν γε ὄντας), who visit his town. To help these is humanity (φιλάν-θρωπον, Fr. 2 and 62). 'For though the various divisions of the earth give each group a different country, the whole circumference of this world gives all men one country, all the earth; and one home, the world' (Fr. 24). Therefore, in the evening of his life, conscious that his efforts will soon be cut short by death, and seeing that the mass of men, like a flock of sheep, still strengthen in one another the deadly plague of false opinions, he 'has decided to make use of this cloister to proffer publicly the medicine of salvation' (τὰ τῆς σωτηρίας φάρμακα, Fr. 2). The medicine is, of course, philosophy, in its two main divisions, laid down by the famous letters of Epicurus, 'physiology' and ethics.

It was seen from the first that the fragments did not all belong to one book. In fact there appear to be fragments of six different works or series contained in our remains. Taking them in the order in which William prints them, they are as follows:

A. *De Natura Rerum Liber* (Fr. 1-14). No title is preserved, but the work is plainly a 'physiology'. It falls into three parts. First there is a general introduction, to which some reference has been already made, setting forth the profits of philosophy and the motives which have led Diogenes to seek to spread the knowledge of it. Next follows a very summary review of previous thought, in the course of which the doctrine is strangely attributed to 'Aristotle and the Peripatetics' that nothing is knowable since all things are in flux (οὐδὲν ἐπιστητόν φασιν εἶναι· ῥεῖν γὰρ αἰεὶ τὰ πράγματα, Fr. 4). Of the criticism of Democritus, which might be interesting, unfortunately very little survives. In general, this section is of no great value. Lastly, the author seems to have developed constructively the views of the Epicureans, ending with an unfinished discussion of the scepticism of Diagoras and Protagoras in regard to the gods. This section contains an account of the origin of men and of the introduction of clothing, speech, and writing (Fr. 10, 11), which affords an interesting comparison with the famous account in the fifth book of Lucretius's poem.

B. *De Innumerabilitate Mundorum* (Fr. 15-21). This is a letter written by Diogenes at Rhodes to a certain Antipater at Athens, in answer to questions received from him concerning the Epicurean doctrine of innumerable worlds. The argument of the letter is difficult to reconstruct, since little of it has survived. The writer sends greetings to friends at Athens, Chalcis, and Thebes.

C. *Disputatio Ethica* (Fr. 22-41). The title survives in a mutilated form, and is reconstructed by William as follows: Διογένους [τοῦ Οἰνο]ανδέως· π[ερὶ τέλους,] παθῶν καὶ [πρά-ξεων] ἐπιτομ[αί]. The introduction (Fr. 23-4) is similar to that of A, and was evidently composed for the Inscription. First, the end, pleasure, is established, with virtue as means to it (not a τέλος itself, as the Stoics, with their foolish fussing over virtue, say) (Fr. 25). This leads to an interesting classification of causes in respect of time as precedent, concomitant, and subsequent (πρωτοχρονεῖ, συγχρονεῖ, μεταχρονεῖ). The instance of the third class is hope or expectation. Virtue is a cause of pleasure in the second sense (Fr. 26). So much, then, of the end.

With Fr. 29 we enter a new chapter dealing with the question how the happy life is to be secured in practice. The writer subdivides the field in which happiness is to be won into καταστήματα and πράξεις, states and actions. This opposition is not found in any other Epicurean source; but it is rash to assume, as many writers do, that it is of Diogenes' invention or due to misunderstanding of what he had heard. Σαρκὸς εὐσταθὲς κατάστημα is a well-attested Epicurean catchword, which goes back to the master himself.[1] Further, Epicurus's distinction between καταστηματικὴ ἡδονή and ἡ ἐν κινήσει[2] might easily have led the school, or some members of it, to treat of pleasure under the two heads of κατάστημα and πρᾶξις. For the 'movement' of a will is an act. The argument against Diogenes' use of the word κατάστημα would be stronger if an instance could be found of an inconsistent use

---

[1] Usener, *Epicurea*, Fr. 68 (see also p. 89, l. 22, and p. 345, ll. 3, 6).

[2] Ib. Fr. 1, 2, 416 (also p. 356, ll. 15 ff.). Cicero translated καταστηματικός *stabilis* or *stans* opp. *movens voluptas*.

in a document of the school. But in fact, apart from the phrase of Epicurus quoted above, the word does not seem to occur at all. What survives of the section dealing with καταστήματα treats of the removal of emotion and fear, i.e. with the freedom from anxiety (ἀταραξία) which. according to Epicurus, was the only καταστηματικὴ ἡδονή. The fear of the gods leads to a discussion of divination (Fr. 31-3), which stands or falls with the belief in fate; and that superstition has been finally refuted by Epicurus's doctrine of the free deviation (κίνησις παρεγκλιτική, κ. ἐλευθέρα) of atoms. This passage is the only surviving statement in Greek of this famous Epicurean doctrine, already known from Lucretius and from Cicero, but it consists of only a few lines, and gives no help in regard to difficulties of detail. The concluding section of our remains (Fr. 34–40) deals with the relation of the soul and the body, presumably in connexion with the fear of death. The views of Pythagoras and Empedocles on transmigration are refuted, as well as the partial belief of the Stoics in the survival of the soul after death. (The theory refuted is that of Chrysippus.) Finally, the superior importance of the soul as compared with the body, and the power of the soul over the body, are emphasized.

No fragments remain of the section dealing with πράξεις ; and another missing section is the discussion of ἀφροσύνη promised in Fr. 25. William calculates [1] that the original treatise contained over a hundred columns, of which only forty-three have survived, even partially.

D. *Epicuri Sententiae* (Fr. 42–61). This γνωμολόγιον was probably intended to illustrate the ethical treatise to which it was appended. There are several other known instances of similar collections of sayings, in addition to the collection of Κύριαι δόξαι preserved by Diogenes Laertius. They were probably formed by extracting notable sayings from the correspondence of the master, and often included sayings of his associates, particularly of Metrodorus. The Oenoanda collection contains at least eight sentences not known from other sources, but familiar in character and no doubt genuine.

[1] Praef., p. xvi.

Fr. 57, which asserts personal independence to be a necessity of happiness, supports this by an instance of the opposite which many will corroborate from recent expeiience—χαλεπὸν στρατεία κἂν ἑτέρων ἀρχῇ.

E. *Scripta Privata* (Fr. 62–66). The most important of these is Fr. 63–4, *Epistula ad Matrem*, which has been thought by many distinguished scholars, including Usener himself, to be a letter from Epicurus to his mother. In his preface William subjects this view to a searching examination and conclusively proves it to be untenable. The letter is no doubt from Diogenes, probably engaged in the study of philosophy at Rhodes, to his mother at home. She has been troubled with dreams, of the nature of which there is a short and difficult discussion. He is happy in philosophy. She (and independently, it seems, his father also) has been sending him money. He begs her to send no more : he is well off and she must not go short on his account.

F. *De Senectute Liber* (Fr. 67–82). The fragments of this work are too ill-preserved to be of much value. Sentences dealing with the pains of age and other familiar topics can be deciphered. If Diels's ingenious restoration is accepted, we have in Fr. 70 the otherwise unknown proverbial expression, ' to shear a sheep with a spear ', used of verbal exaggeration— εἰ μέν τις τὰς ἀμαυρώσεις τῶν γερόντων τυφλώσεις λέ[ξ]ειε, οἶν δό[ρατ]ι πέκοι ἄν: ' in re exigua ', William paraphrases, ' graviore utatur voce '. The phrase is well worth having, though apparently few of the letters preserved are beyond dispute.

Enough remains of Diogenes' work to justify a judgement upon him not only as a teacher but as a writer. He has a considerable power of exposition ; he develops his argument clearly and concisely, and has a certain power of ending his periods effectively. There is a grave earnestness in the opening sentences, summarized above, in which he declares his purpose, and the measured style reflects it :

Τούτους οὖν ὁρῶν (πάλιν γὰρ ἐπαναλήμψομαι) διακειμένους οὕτως, κατωλοφυράμην μὲν αὐτῶν τὸν βίον καὶ ἐπεδάκρυσα τῇ τῶν χρόνων ἀπωλείᾳ, χρηστοῦ δέ τινος ἡγησάμην ἀνδρός, ὅσον ἔστ᾽ ἐφ᾽ ἡμεῖν ... [βοηθεῖν] (Fr. 1. ii). 'Ἐπεὶ δέ, ὡς προεῖπα, οἱ πλεῖστοι καθάπερ ἐν λοιμῷ τῇ περὶ τῶν πραγμάτων ψευδοδοξίᾳ νοσοῦσι κοινῶς. γείνονται δὲ καὶ πλείονες (διὰ γὰρ τὸν ἀλλήλων ζῆλον ἄλλος ἐξ ἄλλου λαμβάνει τὴν νόσον, ὡς τὰ πρόβατα),[1] δίκαιο[ν δ᾽ ἐστὶ καὶ] τοῖς μεθ᾽ ἡμᾶς ἐσομένοις βοηθῆσαι (κἀκεῖνοι γάρ εἰσιν ἡμέτεροι καὶ εἰ [μὴ] γεγόνασί πω), πρὸς δὲ δὴ φιλάνθρωπον καὶ τοῖς παραγεινομένοις ἐπικουρεῖν ξένοις ... ἠθέλησα τῇ στοᾷ ταύτῃ καταχρησάμενος ἐν κοινῷ τὰ τῆς σωτηρίας προθε[ῖναι φάρμα]κα (Fr. 1. iv). And again (Fr. 2. ii, iii) 'Ἐπὶ δυ]σμαῖς γὰρ ἤδη τοῦ βίου καθεστηκότες διὰ τὸ γῆρας, καὶ ὅσον οὔπω μέλλοντες ἀναλύειν ἐκ τοῦ ζῆν ... ἠθελήσαμεν, ἵνα μὴ προλη`μφθῶμεν, βοηθεῖν ἤδη τοῖς εὐσυγκρίτοις (probably 'men of understanding' or 'judgement').

He puts his points pithily : καθ᾽ ἑκάστην μὲν γὰρ ἀποτομὴν τῆς γῆς ἄλλων ἄλλη πατρίς ἐστιν, κατὰ δὲ τὴν ὅλην περιοχὴν τοῦδε τοῦ κόσμου μία πάντων πατρίς ἐστιν ἡ πᾶσα γῆ, καὶ εἷς ὁ κόσμος οἶκος (Fr. 24. i). And in the letter to his mother (Fr. 64. ii) οὐ γὰρ σοί τι βούλομαι λείπειν (' any deficiency ') ἵν᾽ ἐμοὶ περιττεύῃ, λείπειν δ᾽ ἐμοὶ μᾶλλον, ἵνα μὴ σοί.

No doubt, as William abundantly shows in his introduction, his diction is Hellenistic, and his constructions are not Attic (πλήν for ἀλλά, καίτοι with the participle, μή for οὐ,² and even the vulgar form ὀχί for οὐχί occurs) ;[2] yet his terminology is not so cumbrous, nor his sentences so lumbering, as Plutarch's, even if they are not as polished as those of a highly trained rhetorician like Dion of Prusa, or as easy as those of a popularizer like Hierocles. The style of his preaching has the ring of sincerity.   J. L. S.

The Later Stoicism : Hierocles.

A large fragment of a treatise on the Stoic philosophy, the 'Ἠθικὴ Στοιχείωσις of Hierocles, a teacher of the first century A. D., in the reign of Hadrian, was published in 1906.[3]

---

[1] ἐν λοιμῷ and ὡς τὰ πρόβατα recall Thucydides' description of the plague : ὥσπερ τὰ πρόβατα ἔθνησκον, ii. 51. 4.

[2] His mistakes in calling Empedocles 'ὁ 'Ἀκράγου', 'the son of Acragas' (Fr. 5, col. ii), and in attributing Heraclitus's ' Flux ' to Aristotle (Fr. 4, col ii), show that his historical training was imperfect.

[3] Berlin Papyrus 9780, in Berlin. Klass. Texte, vol. iv, edited by von Arnim.

A philosopher named Hierocles had long been known from a large number of excerpts preserved by Stobaeus. These are concerned with the religious and moral duties of man (περὶ καθηκόντων) under titles such as πῶς θεοῖς χρηστέον, πῶς συγγενέσι χρηστέον, πῶς πατρίδι χρηστέον. The opinion current among scholars till 1906 was that these excerpts were from the work of a neo-Platonist philosopher of the fifth century who was a pupil of Plutarch, and who is best known as the author of a Commentary on the χρυσᾶ ἔπη of the pseudo-Pythagoras. In that year, however, Praechter published a critical examination of the excerpts, in which he maintained that they were of much earlier date than had hitherto been assumed, and were probably to be attributed to a Stoic philosopher named Hierocles, a contemporary of Epictetus, who is mentioned as *vir sanctus et gravis* in Aulus Gellius, ix. 5. 8.

This fortunate conjecture became a certainty through the discovery of the Papyrus. The new text agrees sufficiently in style and treatment with the excerpts to make it impossible to doubt that both come from the same hand; and as the Papyrus belongs to the second century, the author cannot be the neo-Platonist of the fifth. Von Arnim would go farther, and is of the opinion that both are fragments of the same treatise. Here it may be doubted if he has said the last word. There seems to be a difference in rhythm between the new fragment and the excerpts. The style of the fragment is rather arid and businesslike, but that of the excerpts is supple and varied, as if addressed to a more popular audience. In particular the ditrochaic or epitrite endings, e. g. συμβίωσις, γηροβοσκούς, which are rather marked in the excerpts, are by no means so common in the fragment. Yet both are clearly akin, as if written by the same man at a different time or for a different purpose. This suspicion is enforced by the subject-matter of the fragment. If fragment and excerpts are from one and the same book, it is strange that the same doctrine should be stated in scientific terms at the opening of the treatise, and then restated in popular language towards the end without any reference to the previous statement. For instance, in the fragment we have an elaboration of the Stoic

doctrine of οἰκείωσις, well known from Diog. Laer. vii. 85.
Man's progress in morality consists in adapting himself to
ever-widening spheres of conduct. Sensation enables him to
adapt himself to his own body (οἰκειοῦται ἑαυτῷ καὶ τῇ ἑαυτοῦ
συστάσει). By the same process of 'adaptation' he enters
into moral relations with his family and kin, with his native
land, and finally with humanity. So far the fragment. But
when we turn to the excerpt in Stob. Fl. 84. 23 (von Arnim,
p. 61. 10), which deals with the question πῶς συγγενέσι
χρηστέον, we have the matter popularly expounded through
the obvious simile of a point surrounded with concentric
circles, with never a hint of the doctrine of οἰκείωσις. Yet if
both passages belong to the same book, we should surely
expect the scientific explanation to be echoed in the popular
exposition.

The new fragment is of great interest as a specimen of a
treatise on Stoic morality belonging to the first century. It
is a popular handbook for the educated layman rather than
a primer of elements for the beginner. The illustrations given
are nearly always happy, and are often both curious and
amusing. Take the story of the bear, which is used to illustrate the doctrine that the animal has sensation of itself as
a whole. It has this sensation since it is aware of the value
and function of the different parts of its body (col. 2. 27 sqq.):
' Thus the bear knows that her head is particularly vulnerable.[1]
She therefore protects her head with her paws from blows that
may prove dangerous. If she is pursued by the hunter, she saves
herself by her powers of leaping, in which she can compare with
any animal of her own size. If, however, she is confronted by a
chasm which she judges to be too broad for a flying leap (δια-
λέσθαι), she flings herself down to the bottom. But she does not
fling herself anyhow (ῥιπτεῖ δ' οὐχ ὡς ἔτυχεν). She inflates herself
to her full extent, and after making herself as much like a balloon
as possible (κατὰ τὸ ἐνδεχόμενον ἀσκῷ ποιήσασα πεπνευματω-
μένῳ παραπλησίαν), goes slithering down the slope (κατα-
φέρεται), keeping her legs and head off the ground, and con-
triving to break her fall by means of the inflated portions of

[1] Cf. Pliny, N. H. xi. 48.

her body.' Or take again the observation upon children, which serves to illustrate the animal instinct for self-preservation (col. 7. 5 sqq.): 'This seems to be the reason why young children cannot bear to be shut up in a dark house where there is not a sound to be heard. They exert their organs of sense, and, being unable to see or hear anything, form the impression that they have ceased to exist, and so become uneasy. This is why competent nurses recommend their charges to close their eyes (διὸ καὶ φιλοτέχνως αἱ τίτθαι παρεγγυῶσιν αὐτοῖς ἐπιμύειν τοὺς ὀφθαλμούς). It assuages their terror to feel that the absence of objects of sight is due to their own act rather than to necessity.'

The fragment does not add much to our knowledge of Stoic theory. The language in which the theory was embodied had long become common form. Thus the application of the doctrine of the κρᾶσις δι' ὅλου to the relation between soul and body is given in col. 4. 4, as follows:[1] 'The soul is not contained in the body as in a vessel, like liquids held in jars, but is compounded and blended with the body in a mysterious way, so that even the tiniest fragment of the compound is not without its share in either of the component parts.

[1] This last fragment reminds us of the remarkable poem *Nosce Teipsum*, 'On the Soul of Man and the Immortality thereof', by Sir John Davies, published in 1599, in which the idea is elaborated:

> But how shall we this union well express?
> Nought ties the soul: her subtilty is such
> She moves the body, which she doth possess,
> Yet no part toucheth, but by Virtue's touch.
>
> Then dwells she not therein as in a tent,
> Nor as a pilot in his ship doth sit;
> Nor as the spider in her web is pent;
> Nor as the wax retains the print in it;
>
> Nor as a vessel water doth contain;
> Nor as one liquor in another shed;
> Nor as the heat doth in the fire remain;
> Nor as a voice throughout the air is spread:
>
> But as the fair and cheerful morning light
> Doth here and there her silver beams impart,
> And in an instant doth herself unite
> To the transparent air, in all, and part:
>
> So doth the piercing soul the body fill,
> Being all in all, and all in part diffused;
> Indivisible, incorruptible still,
> Not forced, encountered, troubled or confused. Sect. X.

This blend is very like what takes place in the case of molten iron; for there, just as here, the juxtaposition of the components is found in every part of the compound.' Here not only the technical terms, but the metaphors also, had already been formulated by the school, and were known to us from the works of Alexander Aphrodisiensis, who, though later in date than Hierocles, must have derived them from the writings of the founders.

Hierocles is a compiler, and it is unfortunate that the Papyrus is defective at the very point where he is beginning a quotation from Chrysippus (col. 8. 10). He worked upon the long series of treatises which he inherited from his predecessors, and although he is not original, his treatise has its place among those which preserved the teaching of the great founders of the Stoic school.   F. W. H.

Note on the Contents of the Library at Herculaneum.[1]

The following further details as to the contents of the Herculaneum Library may be of use. Pap. 1251 contains an interesting moral tract, attributed by Comparetti to Epicurus himself, but probably by Philodemus (? part of the περὶ θανάτου). It was published by Comparetti in *Museo Italiano di antichità classica*, 1884 (comment and corrections by Usener, *Epicurea*, pp. xlvi ff.). Another moral tract (Pap. 831), certainly belonging to the early days of the school, is attributed by Körte with some probability to Metrodorus and printed by him at the end of his collection of the fragments of M. Polystratus has been dealt with above. Apart from these the most important new Epicurean contribution is that of Demetrius Lacon (fl. c. 120 B.C.: see Crönert, *Kol. u. Men.*, pp. 122 ff.). Specimens will also be found in Crönert's work of Colotes, Carneïscus, and Nicasicrates.

Of the περὶ φύσεως of Epicurus the chief published restorations are these. Bks. II and XI—Orelli (as above). Bks. XI and XIV—Gomperz, *Zeitschr. für d. Oest. Gymnasien*, 1867. Bk. XI—Mancini, *Atti del Congresso Internaz. di Scienze storiche*, ii. 249 (1905). Bk. XXVIII—Cosattini, *Hermes*, 29 (1894). An unnumbered book discusses freedom of the will: Gomperz, *Wiener Studien*, i (1880) J. L. S. Another (on generation): Cosattini, *Riv. di Filol.* 20 (1892). Isolated passages from these and other books—Gomperz: 'Neue Bruchstücke Epikurs' in *Sitz. d. Wiener Akad.* 83 (1876). Of the following Papyri, which are thought to belong to this work, no published restoration (apart from isolated passages) is available:—P. Herc. 362, 419, 454, 989, 996, 1054, 1116, 1151 (Bk. XV), 1199, 1385 (Bk. XX), 1398, 1420, 1431, 1489, 1634, 1639. But many of these are not likely to yield anything of importance.

Lastly, special interest attaches to the unpublished Pap. 1413, a dialogue concerning Time, probably by Epicurus. For this see Crönert, *Kol. u. Men.*, p. 104, note 501.   J. L. S.

---

[1] See p. 28.

I I

L Y R I C P O E T R Y

(i) *Hieratic*

The Paean, The Hymn.

OUR knowledge of Lyric Poetry has lately been increased
by additions from two sources, Inscriptions and Papyri, and
since the Inscriptions are in better preservation and give us
longer and complete poems, they will be treated of first.
They form additions to our knowledge of Greek religious
Ritual and Ceremonial. It is better to use this expression
rather than 'Greek Religion', or 'the poetry of Greek Religion',
and thus avoid falling into the mistake which some recent
writers have made, of treating religion and ceremonial as if
they were the same thing.

The Hymns (to use the term 'Hymn' in its generic sense)
which will be considered, illustrate temple ceremonial rather
than religious ideas, for which we must go to the great poets ;
and although they cannot rank among the higher efforts of
the Greek religious genius, they have their place in the
history of the language, metre, dialect, and conspicuously
music.

Matthew Arnold [1] once said of a collection of Hymns made
by an eminent public man of the day, that 'so far as poetry
was concerned', it was 'a monument of a nation's weakness'.
He was referring rather to the effect of putting dogmatic
phraseology into verse ; and perhaps if we were to judge only
by the Orphic Hymns, the Dithyrambs, and the strange
'Hymns' of Callimachus, laboriously compiled, it would seem,
out of a handbook of mythology and a Dialect Dictionary,
and containing not enough religion (to borrow the expression
of a celebrated Bishop) 'to save a tomtit', we should say the
same of any similar Greek collection.

[1] *The Study of Celtic Literature*, vi.

In the hand of a master, a religious poem may show great
beauty, as the Hyporchema, which is akin to the Paean, in
Sophocles' *Ajax*, 693 sqq., a merry hymn to Pan ; or the richly
wrought and glowing Hyporchema to Dionysus, in *Antigone*
1146 sqq. :

> ἰὼ πῦρ πνειόντων χοράγ' ἄστρων, νυχίων
> φθεγμάτων ἐπίσκοπε

just as in the hands of a religious thinker like Cleanthes it
may be solemn and elevated. The worst charge that can be
made against poems of this kind is that they are apt to be
cut and dried in form, as in Aristophanes' *Thesmophoriazusae*,
107 sqq., just as we are aware of a certain conventionality and
formality in the Paeans now before us.

One religious Paean (for that it is a Paean to Apollo is
shown by the concluding words) of an earlier age has been
preserved for us in the great Papyrus of Bacchylides XVI
(Theseus). It is of singular beauty. There is another which
we would wish had been preserved : Alcaeus's Paean, of which
Himerius [1] gives a prose paraphrase.

Hymns found at Delphi.

(1) The *Paean of Philodamus* [2] in honour of Dionysus was
found by French scholars in 1894 at Delphi. Philodamus
belonged to Scarpheia, a small town in Locris near Ther-
mopylae, and the date at which he wrote, 328 B.C., can be
determined with some accuracy, since an accompanying
Inscription records the name of the Archon in whose year of
office (either 339–338 or 331–330 B.C.) a vote of the Delphians
was passed in honour of the author of the Hymn.

It shows ease of expression and command of technique.
The author evidently enjoyed his subject, and spun it out to
some 160 lines, more than 100 of which are preserved.

The material structure is elegant. It contained twelve

[1] Orat. xvi. 10; Bergk, *P. L. G.* Alc. Fr.
[2] *Bull. Corr. Hell.* xix. 393 sqq., 548 ; xxi. 510 sqq.; A. Fairbanks, *A
Study of the Greek Paean*, Cornell Studies in Classical Philology, No. xii
(1900).

strophes based upon the pleasing Glyconic metre which Sophocles employed in some of his most characteristic Odes.[1]

The fifth line in every stanza is a Refrain ($M\epsilon\sigma\acute{v}\mu\nu\iota ov$) in Ionic *a minori* metre, and the seventh is a Phalaecean. The last three lines form a ' Burden ' ('$E\phi\acute{v}\mu\nu\iota ov$). The effect of this metrical variety is bright and pleasing, and gives a sense of free and joyous movement. This material structure clearly points to an antiphon between the leader of the chorus and the main body who interpose with refrain and burden. The musical notation was not added, as it is to the two Delphian Hymns which will be treated of below.

The Paean was meant to be sung, not before an altar, but by a procession on its way through the streets.

The subject is the birth of Dionysus at Thebes, his epiphany on Parnassus, the honours given to him at the Eleusinian Mysteries ; his visit to the cities of Thessaly and the Pierian shrine on Olympus, where Apollo led the chorus of the Muses, and saluted him as ' Glorious Paean '. Then came, in a passage not preserved, the command of the oracle to complete some work connected with the temple ; to perform the hymn, and institute sacrifices. Finally the glory of the completed temple with its golden statues is described ; sacrifices are to be offered and dances performed in his honour at the Pythian Games, and a statue of the god is to be set in a car drawn by golden lions, and a cave to be prepared meet for him.

(2) *Limenius's Hymn to Apollo.*[2] The discovery in 1893 by French scholars of large fragments of two Hymns was of unusual interest and importance, since they were, and still are, the longest known pieces with musical notation ; in one case, the Hymn of Limenius, instrumental, in the other, by an unknown author, vocal.

The name of Limenius (a Citharoedus, ' son of Thoinos ') was cleverly detected by M. Colin on the fragmentary dedication, and is certain. The Hymn is composed in the Lydian mode, and is furnished with an instrumental score. The metre is

---

[1] *O. T.* 1185 sqq. ; *O. C.* 1210 sqq.
[2] *Fouilles de Delphes*, iii, Fasc. ii, p. 158. We follow the arrangement of the fragments of the stone by MM. Colin and Reinach.

Paeonic, or, more strictly, Cretic resolved into Paeonic, a metre suited to the movement of a lively dance. It is loosely constructed in style, but contains a pretty description of the joy of the heavens and the calm of air and sea when Apollo was born :

πᾶς δὲ γάθησε πόλος οὐράνιος . . .
νηνέμους δ' ἔσχεν αἰθὴρ ἀε[λλῶν ταχυπετεῖς] δρόμους·
λῆξε δὲ βαρυβρόμου Νη[ρέως ζαμενὲς ο]ἶδμ'
ἠδὲ μέγας 'Ωκεανός, ὃς πέριξ [γᾶν ὑγραῖς ἀγ]κάλαις ἀμπέχει.

There is a fragmentary reference to the invasion of the Gauls under Brennus in 279–8 B.C., when they were miraculously repulsed in a snowstorm. The story is in Pausanias,[1] and was the great event in later Delphian history. Echoes of the invasion are heard in Callimachus,[2] and in a recently discovered fragment of an Elegiac poem which will be dealt with below, as well as in the anonymous Hymn which follows. It concludes with a prayer in Glyconics to Apollo and Artemis for prosperity, and for the preservation of the Roman power. This is important for fixing the date, which is probably between 138 and 128 B.C. A noteworthy feature in this Hymn and the next is the fact that when a long vowel or diphthong is sung to two musical notes, it is written twice,[3] as ὕμνωων, κλειειτύν, αἰθηήρ.

It is also noticeable that the performers are not trained amateur citizens, as they would have been in the old days, but professional artists : ἱερὸς (sc. ἐσμός which occurs in the next Hymn) τεχνιτῶν ἔνοικος πόλει Κεκροπία, and τεχνιτωῶν is probably to be restored in the following Hymn. The great number of new festivals[4] instituted in the third century led to the rapid increase of guilds of artists who travelled from city to city. They were in the first instance Dionysiac artists, but afterwards their performances were not confined to Dionysiac

---

[1] Paus. x. 23.   [2] H. in Del. 173 sqq.
[3] Contrast the greater freedom of εἰειει ιλίσσετε in Aristoph. Ran. 1314. But in Eur. Electr. 437 the later hand of L has εἰειλισσόμενος, and the Rainer Papyrus of Eur. Orest. 343 gives ὥως, with two notes in the vocal notation (Jan, Mus. Scr. Gr. ii, p. 430.
[4] See the list in W. S. Ferguson, Hellenistic Athens, p. 296, and Index, s. v. ' Technitae '.

festivals. The development of this profession would not have pleased Plato, who would have had his citizens take their own parts in the monthly [1] festival throughout the year, with sacrifices, choruses, and musical and gymnastic contests.

(3) *The Anonymous Delphian Hymn to Apollo*.[2] This was formerly, on the strength of a Delphian Inscription of about 216–215 B.C., attributed to Cleochares, an Athenian, who had composed ποθόδιόν τε καὶ Παιᾶνα καὶ ὕμνον to Apollo; but this inscription is now thought to refer to a composition older than this Hymn.[3] The author's name has disappeared from the stone; but he was an Athenian, and the Hymn is of the same date as the preceding. It is composed in the Phrygian mode, partly diatonic, partly chromatic. The metre, like that of Limenius's Hymn, is Cretic resolved into Paeonic. The composer writes with fluency and freedom, and evidently took delight in the ceremony. He gives a vivid picture of the sacrifice burning on the altar; the cloud of Arabian incense spreading up to the sky; the clear notes of the flute, the sweet sound of the golden harp blending with the voices:

ἀγίοις δὲ βω-
μοῖσιν Ἄφαιστος αἴθει νέων μῆρα ταύ-
ρων· ὁμοῦ δέ νιν Ἄραψ ἀτμὸς ἐς Ὄλυμπον ἀνακίδναται,
λιγὺ δὲ λωτὸς βρέμων αἰόλοις μέλεσιν ᾠδὰν κρέκει·
χρύσεα δ' ἀδύθρους κίθαρις ὕμνοισιν ἀναμέλπεται.

The language is simple, and the picture is as clear as the bright air in which the rite was performed. Aeschylus treats a similar scene rather with language of dignity and splendour:

εὔφαμον δ' ἐπὶ βωμοῖς
μοῦσαν θείατ' ἀοιδοί·
ἀγνῶν τ' ἐκ στομάτων φερέ-
σθω φάμα φιλοφόρμιγξ.[4]

After this picture follow the mythical deeds of the god, as in the Hymn of Limenius; his destruction of the Old Serpent of Delphi, and the repulse of the Gauls: Γαλατᾶν Ἄρης ἄσεπτος.

(4, 5) *The Paeans of Aristonous of Corinth.* We have two

---

[1] *Laws* viii. 828 B.   [2] *Fouilles de Delphes*, iii, pt. ii, p. 150.
[3] Ib., p. 163.   [4] Aesch. *Suppl.* 694.

Paeans by Aristonous of Corinth, found by the French scholars at Delphi; one to Apollo[1] and one to Hestia.[2] They are written in the conventional style, with nothing remarkable in the language; but the single ornamental epithets are used with precision and good taste. Such Hymns could be turned off by any facile writer. The Paean to Apollo is written in careful Glyconics; that to Hestia is of the Enoplian type. The opening of the Paean to Apollo is very like the opening lines of Aeschylus's *Eumenides*, and the language of that to Hestia is like Euripides' Ode in the *Ion*, 461 sqq. But it is not necessary to suppose that the writer was indebted to these poets; rather all three drew from a common source, their own knowledge of the ceremonies of Delphi.

From the mention of the Archon Damochares in the official inscription which precedes the Paean to Apollo, the date is now thought to be 222 B.C.

The Paean of Isyllus of Epidaurus.

This Paean to Asclepius[3] was found inscribed on a stone at the Asclepieion of Epidaurus, the chief centre of the worship of Asclepius, and a hospital conducted by priests. Readers of Aristophanes' *Plutus* will remember the amusing description of a night spent in it by a blind patient, and how, when all was quiet, the priest came round and 'consecreted the offerings into a bag' (ἥγιζεν ἐς σάκταν τινά[4]).

Isyllus gives some information about himself in some Hexameters which follow his Paean. He came as a sick boy from Bousporus or Bosporus, probably a town near Epidaurus, at the time when 'Philip was leading an army against Sparta to destroy royalty'. He was met by Asclepius, in flashing armour. 'Have pity on me, Asclepius,' he cried. The deity replied: 'Courage! In due time will I come to thee when I have saved Sparta, because they righteously observe the oracles

[1] Colin in *Fouilles de Delphes*, iii, Fasc. pt. ii, p. 215; Collitz, ii, No. 2721.
[2] Colin in *Fouilles de Delphes*, iii, Fasc. pt. ii, p. 217.
[3] Collitz-Bechtel, 3342; Wilamowitz-Moellendorff, in *Philolog. Untersuchungen*, ix, Berlin, 1886.
[4] Aristoph. *Plut.* 681.

of Phoebus which Lycurgus enjoined upon them.' Some time
after this Isyllus inscribed his Paean. Two dates have been
proposed for it. Wilamowitz thinks that the reference is to
the march of Philip of Macedon against Sparta after the battle
of Chaeronea in 338 B.C.; Blass and Bechtel think that it
refers to the invasion of Philip V in 218 mentioned by Polybius;[1]
but the style of the lettering points to the earlier date.
Isyllus was then a boy, so this would put his *floruit* about
300 B.C. He appears to have caused an ordinance to be
passed that the noblest men of the city should go in procession, ' with hair flowing down ', to the temples of Apollo and
Asclepius, and pray that the blessings of upright dealing,
good laws, peace, health, and wealth may be granted to
Epidaurus. Then follows the Paean. It is poetically poor.
It contains no moral idea, and the expression is commonplace,
rude, and wooden ; the genealogy of Asclepius is merely given,
and the Paean ends with the ordinary prayer for the prosperity
and health of the city. It is written in the Ionic *a minori*
metre, with frequent anaclasis ($- \cup - \cup$ for $\cup \cup - -$). Wilamowitz,
who has analysed the metre, thinks that Isyllus used the
metre of the fourth-century Attic Dithyramb without recognizing its unfitness for a hymn used in worship. The Ionic
a minori is a loose and relaxing metre, and although suitable
for a hymn to Bacchus, as in Aristoph. *Ran.* 324, is out of place
in a Paean to Asclepius.

The chief value of the Paean consists in the addition which
it makes to our knowledge of the dialect of Epidaurus.

The Paean to Asclepius from Ptolemais, Dium, and Athens.

The Erythraean Paean to Asclepius,[2] of which the date is
about 360 B.C., is almost identical with that from Ptolemais
(Menschieh) in Egypt,[3] of Trajan's time. There is also a fragment of the same Paean at Athens,[4] and lately another copy,
like that of Ptolemais, has come to light at Caritza, the
ancient Dium,[5] in Macedonia. It is written in Dactylic

[1] Polyb. v. 18 sqq.   [2] Wilamowitz, *Nordionische Steine*, 1909, p. 38.
[3] Baillet, *Rev. Arch.*, 1889, p. 70.   [4] *I. G.* iii. 171 C, p. 490.
[5] G. Oikonomos, Ἐπιγραφαὶ τῆς Μακεδονίας, i: Athens, 1915.

Dimeters, and is of the conventional type: a genealogy of the god and a concluding prayer. The language contains nothing remarkable, but a comparison with the other copies reveals points of some interest. The copy from Ptolemais can be dated almost exactly: it is between A.D. 98, the first year of Trajan's reign, and 103; but not after 103, because the title Dacicus, which he assumed in that year, does not appear in the accompanying dedicatory inscription. The copy from Dium is a little later. Strangely enough, these two copies appear to be better than the earlier, for in the prayer occur the words

$$\delta\grave{o}s \ \delta' \ \dot{\eta}\mu\hat{a}s \ \chi a\acute{\iota}\rho o\nu\tau as \ \dot{o}\rho\hat{a}\nu \ \phi\acute{a}os$$
$$\text{'}H\epsilon\lambda\acute{\iota}o\upsilon \ \delta o\kappa\acute{\iota}\mu o\upsilon s \ \sigma\grave{\upsilon}\nu \ \dot{a}\gamma a\kappa\lambda\upsilon\tau\hat{\omega}$$
$$\epsilon\dot{\upsilon}a\gamma\epsilon\hat{\iota} \ \text{'}\Upsilon\gamma\iota\epsilon\acute{\iota}a.$$

Here δοκίμους is used in a correct and technical sense, *spectatos*, 'tried and approved', literally 'after passing medical tests'; but the earlier Erythraean copy has δόκιμον, which must go with φάος, and then makes no sense, however hard Wilamowitz may struggle with it. Again, the late copy for Ptolemais has μιχθεὶς ἐν φιλότητι Κορωνίδι τᾷ Φλεγυείᾳ, which appears also to have stood on the Athenian copy, while that from Dium has Κορωνίδι τῇ Φλεγύαο, and the Erythraean Κορωνίδι ἐν γᾷ τᾷ Φλεγυείᾳ. Now the expression Κορωνίδι τᾷ Φλεγυείᾳ means 'Coronis, the daughter of Phlegyas', and M. Oikonomos has called attention to the fact that this use of the patronymic adjective is a special feature of Northern Greek style.[1] Inscriptions show that it is peculiarly Thessalian. But the author of the copy from Dium (who ought to have known better, being a Northern Greek) gives in a straightforward way Κορωνίδι τῇ Φλεγύαο, and the author of the Erythraean copy appears simply not to have understood τᾷ Φλεγυείᾳ, for he writes ἐν γᾷ τᾷ Φλεγυείᾳ, with excellent sense, but obliterating a local mint-mark; for the worship of Asclepius came from the north, and Tricca in Macedonia was an old, perhaps the oldest, centre of it.

---

[1] Thumb, *Griech. Dial.* s. 226, 227, 4; cf. Riddell on *Odyssey* γ 190 Φιλοκτήτην Ποιάντιον ἀγλαὸν υἱόν.

There is another curious thing. The prayer in the Ery-
threan copy opens with the words

χαῖρέ μοι, ἵλαος δ᾽ ἐπινίσεο
τὰν ἐμὰν πόλιν εὐρύχορον·

which is not very good metrically (did he mean ἀμάν?). Now
the Ptolemaic copy has ἀμετέραν πόλιν εὐρύχορον, which looks
at first sight better, but is not really, because of the hiatus
between ἐπινίσεο and ἀμετέραν. The copy from Dium gets into
a still greater metrical difficulty with Δείων πόλιν εὐρύχορον.
What this appears to point to is, that copies of an appropriate Paean to Asclepius could be supplied from some centre
for the use of any city which required one, with a blank left
for the name of the city to be filled up as was required. No
doubt, if the Athenian copy was complete, we should find
something like Ἀτθίδα Κεκροπίαν πόλιν, which we find in the
Athenian Paean of Macedonius.[1]

Hymn to the Idaean Dactyls.

It is greatly to be wished that the Hymn [2] to these obscure
minor daemons was more completely preserved. It is of the
end of the fourth century B.C., and was found at Eretria in
Euboea. The Idaean Dactyls were daemons associated with
metallurgy, and it is not strange that there should have been
a cult of them at Eretria, for Eretria was near the Lelantine
Plain, where Strabo [3] says that there was the unique occurrence of a mine containing copper and iron.

The Hymn is remarkable, because it contains the earliest
reference to the combination of the worship of Magna Mater
and that of the Idaean Dactyls. The *locus classicus* in literature for this combination is Apollonius Rhodius, *Arg.* i.
1125 sqq., where the locality mentioned is the country of the

---

[1] It is, I think, very doubtful if the Hendecasyllables on Sarapis in the
Archiv f. Religionswiss. xviii [1915], 257-68, are of the Hellenistic age,
much less of the early Hellenistic age, as A. Abt thinks. Mr. Walter
Scott would put them as late as the third century A.D. See H. I. Bell in
the *Journal of Egyptian Archaeology*, vol. vi, part ii, p. 121 (April 1920).
[2] *I. G.* xii. 9, No. 259.   [3] Strabo x. 9.

Doliones, on the south coast of the Euxine. The Scholiast
on the passage adds a parallel instance from Miletus, and the
worship of both, although it is not certain that they were
combined, is found at Epidaurus.[1] The right-hand portion of
the stone that contains the Hymn is broken away, but enough
remains to show that the metre, which is rather rough, was
Dactylic, and apparently Trimeter.

First comes the genealogy of the Dactyls, which is noticeable, since their father, or forefather, is one Eurytheus, a new
name, apparently that of the culture-hero, or the Prometheus, of
Eretria ; for, says the Hymn, he was the first to discover medi-
cinal drugs, was the first physician, and was the first to plant
fruit-trees. Then follows more genealogy; then the transference
of the cult from Crete εἰς Φρυγίαν κώμαν, and finally the references turn to the Mother. Here the fracture of the stone is
particularly tantalizing, because there was evidently a story
how she ἔμβαλε μηνίσασα [νοῦσον or the like], apparently on
account of some duty unperformed : and lastly a reference to the
mixing of wolves' blood, and to the tools of the smith's craft.

J. U. P.

The Hymn of the Kouretes.

A very interesting inscription, about thirty-six lines long
and in good preservation, was discovered in 1903 at Palai-
kastro near Mount Dicte in Eastern Crete. It was found by
Professor Bosanquet among the débris of a Hellenic temple
which had been built on the ruins of an old Minoan town.
The temple must have been that of Zeus Diktaios, known to
us from other sources as a subject of dispute and arbitration
between the towns of Praisos and Itana in the year 139 B.C.[2]
And the inscription is apparently a προσόδιον ; that is, a song
to be sung by a procession marching, or rather dancing,
towards an altar. It is written in continuous Ionic *a maiori*
or quasi-trochaic stanzas with a refrain.

' Io, Kouros Most Great, I give thee hail, Kronian, lord of
all that is wet and gleaming (παγκρατὲς γάνους[3]), thou art

---

[1] Cavvadias, *Fouilles d'Épidaure*, Nos. 64 and 40.
[2] Dittenberger, *Sylloge*[2], ii. 929.
[3] Whether the reading should be γάνος or γάνους is uncertain.

come at the head of thy daimones. To Dikte for the year,
Oh, march and rejoice in the dance and song ($\mu o\lambda\pi\dot{\eta}$),
  That we make to thee with harps and pipes mingled
together, and sing as we come to a stand at thy fenced altar.
  For here the shielded Nurturers took thee, a babe im-
mortal, from Rhea, and with noise of beating feet hid thee
away.

. . . .

  And the seasons began to be fruitful year by year, and
Justice to possess mankind, and all wild living things were
compassed about by wealth-loving Peace.
  [1] To us also leap for full jars, and leap for fleecy flocks, and
leap for fields of fruit and for hives to bring increase.
  Leap for our Cities, and leap for our sea-borne ships, and
leap for young citizens and for goodly law.'

The letters of the inscription can hardly be earlier than the
year 200 A. D.; but they were copied from something older
and apparently difficult ; for the stonemason tried first one
face of the stone, and there made so many mistakes that he
turned the stone over and re-cut the Hymn on the opposite
face. The original however cannot have been pre-classical, nor
even classical ; for the language is a cultured poetical *Koine*,
with some ornamental Dorisms, to give local colour. It
cannot be older than the fourth century B. C.   The same
date is also suggested by the substance of the song.   The
' shielded nurturers ', or Kouretes, are conceived as founders
of the arts of civilization and social progress, a conception
which did not prevail till after the time of Aristotle, and may
be seen at its strongest in Diodorus. Yet, below the post-
Christian lettering and the Hellenistic language, the Hymn
reveals to us a well-known primitive religious ritual and belief.
The repeated ' leaping ' for special emphasis in the course of
the magic dance reminds us of the leaping of the Roman
Salii, who are identified with the Kouretes by Dionysius of
Halicarnassus, *Ant. Rom.* ii. 70. We may compare also the
phrases *limen sali : sta : berber*, and *triumpe triumpe triumpe*,
in the song of the Fratres Arvales.[2]
  The current story about the Curetes in manuals of mytho-

----

[1] The restoration of these two lines is conjectural.
[2] See C. Bailey's Ovid, *Fasti* iii, Introd. p. 44.

logy is, that, when Zeus was an infant, his mother Rhea concealed him from the child-eating Kronos by the help of the Curetes, who danced in full armour round the baby, clashing their weapons so as to drown the noise of his cries, or else so as to frighten Kronos out of the neighbourhood. The story shows the kind of silliness which so often betrays an unexplained ritual origin. The clue to it lies in the wide-spread custom of initiation which we know to have been practised throughout Greece, and with particular persistency in Crete. Initiation is the admission, normally about the age of puberty, of the boys or girls of the tribe into the full status of men or women. The male initiations, with which we are here concerned, were usually accompanied by ordeals of courage or endurance, and took the form of first removing the ' child ' from the care of the women, putting away its dress and toys and other childish things, and even symbolically putting an end to its life, and then producing in its stead a quite new creature, a ' man ', dressed in man's dress, wearing man's weapons, and instructed by the proper male authorities in those mysteries which the men of the tribe must know. Social rituals of this sort nearly always reappear as mythological stories. The myth tells that we practise such and such a rite because Zeus once upon a time had such and such an adventure. The truth of course is that we invent the story about Zeus because we practise the rite.

The word *Koures* is a specialized form of *Κοῦρος*, a ' Young Man ' or ' young full-fledged warrior '. The Kouretes are the specialized ' Men ' or ' warriors ' who take the ' child ' from the women and make from it a real Kouros like themselves. They wear men's armour, they dance the war-dance, and they are free to marry. We may note with interest that as civiliza-tion advances they change their character. The initiation is a τελετή, a ' completion '. According to ' Themis ', that Primaeval Custom which is also Law and is so old that it must be Right, the Kouretes do what the complete man does, and as the complete man (τέλειος ἀνήρ) from being chiefly a fighter becomes more conspicuously a counsellor or a com-mercial or agricultural expert, the yelling savages whose war-

dance frightens the bogy who is going to eat the child, or else
simply frightens the child in order to test its courage, become
gradually the upholders of law, shipbuilders, agriculturists, and
bee-keepers.

The 'Kouros Most Great' is of course Zeus. The infant
Zeus has now been initiated and is himself a Kouros, and
naturally the greatest of all Kouroi. The Kouretes are his
πρόπολοι δαίμονες, his Attendants or Retinue. The Kouretes,
Korybantes, Idaean Dactyls, are related to Zeus, or sometimes
to Zagreus, as the Satyrs, Silenoi, Tityroi are to Dionysus, and
as the Telchines to Hephaistos. The parallels are numerous,
though each has its special peculiarities. Most of the Greek
gods pass through the stage of Kouroi, and many, like Apollo,
Hermes, Ares, remain Kouroi for ever. And the trace of the
initiation ceremony is over all of them, and over many of the
goddesses also.

[See *Annual of B. S. A.* xv (1907–8), pp. 309–65: articles
by Bosanquet, J. E. Harrison, and Murray. Also Jebb in
J. H. S. xxiv, (1904), pp. lvi–lviii; J. U. Powell in *Classical
Quarterly*, ix. 143.]   G. M.

A fragment [1] consisting of four Hexameters may be mentioned here, since it refers to ritual, although not lyric in form.
Maidens say how they went, nine in number, to the temple of
Demeter, wearing festal robes and necklaces of ivory. Some
critics, as Blass and Dr. Weir Smyth, have assigned the lines
to Alcman, since the dialect resembles his, and there is the
mention of such a necklace among his fragments.[2] But the
mixture of Aeolic and Doric forms and Doric accents, and the
treatment of one word in two successive lines first with
a Digamma and then without it,

   παῖσαι παρθενικαί, παῖσαι καλὰ ἔμματ' ἐχοίσαι,
   καλὰ μὲν ἔμματ' ἐχοίσαι,

render this unlikely. And although this repetition of a word
(Anaphora) is found in early Greek, it is used sparingly, while
here it occurs twice in two lines, which betrays the imitator.
It is better to assign the lines to an imitator of Alcman living

---

[1] *Oxyrhynchus Papyri*, i, No. 8; Weir Smyth, *Greek Lyric Poetry*, p. 14.
[2] Alcman, 52, Hiller.

in Alexandrian times. The Scholiast on Callimachus's *Hymn to Demeter* (line 1) says that Ptolemy Philadelphus instituted a feast of Demeter with her κάλαθος, and we may well see here the opening of the description of this Alexandrian cult. It is possible, too, that the following lines from a Papyrus:[1]

> βᾶτε βᾶτε κεῖθεν, αἱ δ'
> ἐς τὸ πρόσθεν ὀρόμεναι
> τίς ποθ' ἀ νεᾶνις; ὡς
> εὐπρεπής νιν ἀμπέχει . . .

are from a pseud-Alcmanic Παρθένειον. This suggestion is due to Professor Stuart Jones.

(ii) *Personal Lyric.*

We now pass to a small group of fragments preserved in Papyri, of a rather later date. They are poems of sentiment. The most remarkable of them, and indeed a poem remarkable in itself, is the so-called ' Fragmentum Grenfellianum ', from the name of its discoverer. In length it was about sixty lines, of which forty are preserved, and it is not a 'fragment', but a poem complete in itself. It is a Παρακλαυσίθυρον, largely in Dochmiacs, often of a free type which takes the form of a Choriambus −∪∪− (a metre in this way doubly adapted to express passionate agitation), giving the lament of the 'lacrimans exclusus amator' of Lucretius, but put into a woman's mouth. It gives a vivid and complete picture of a passionate and rejected love. The passion has not the clear penetrating and poignant quality of Sappho, but is gusty and turbid, and reminds one of the picture of hectic passion in Theocritus's Φαρμακεύτρια:[2]

> Ἄστρα φίλα καὶ πότνια Νὺξ συνερῶσά μοι
> παράπεμψον ἔτι με νῦν πρὸς ὃν
> ἡ Κύπρις ἔκδοτον
> ἄγει με χὼ πολὺς
> ἔρως παραλαβών.
> συνοδηγὸν ἔχω τὸ πολὺ πῦρ
> τοὐν ψυχῇ μου καιόμενον.

---

[1] *Oxyrh. Pap.* i, No. 9.
[2] The most recent text is in O. Crusius's *Herondas*[5], p. 129.

Von Christ sees in it an example of a form of lyric popular in the Alexandrian time, the Μαγῳδία or Σιμῳδία, so called from its inventor, Simus of Magnesia, to whom Crusius assigns the poem. It recalls the Cantica of Plautus.[1]

Of much the same date and written in a similar tone, but less passionate, is a lament in Cretics put into the mouth of Helen,[1] probably a lyric complete in itself:

Νῦν δὲ μούναν μ' ἀφεὶς
ἄλοχον, ἄστοργ', ἄπεις,

which is noticeable because it contains a variant, otherwise unknown, of the story of Menelaus and Helen, and quite inconsistent with the version in the *Odyssey*. Helen reproaches Menelaus for deserting her, although he had sacked Troy for her sake.

Marisaeum Melos.[2]

This consists of eight Ionic *a minori* lines inscribed on the door of a temple at Marisa, between Gaza and Jerusalem, about 150 B.C. Two persons after some banter make an assignation:

Ἀνήρ. Ἀλλ' ἐγὼ μὲν ἀποτρέχω, σοὶ δὲ καταλείπω
εὐρυχωρίην πολλήν.
Γυνή. Πρᾶσσ' ὅτι βούλῃ.

It resembles the Λοκρικὸν ᾆσμα in Bergk, *P. L. G.* iii. 665, and Athenaeus,[3] speaking of the 'Locrian Songs', says that Phoenicia was full of poems like them.

Παρακλαυσίθυρον ii.

A fragment of another Παρακλαυσίθυρον[4] of later date is among the Papyri from Tebtunis, and probably comes from a Mime. The phraseology recalls the 'Fragmentum Grenfellianum' and the 'Melos Marisaeum', but it is not certain

---

[1] The same subject is treated in a fragment of a later date (second century A.D.), *Rylands Pap.* i. 15, with a strophical arrangement: a forsaken girl complains to a gladiator, μορβίλλων (= *mirmillo*) μόνην μ' ἔλιπες.

[2] Crusius, *Herondas*[5], p. 129.   [3] xv. 679 B.   [4] Ib., p. 135.

that it is in verse : the apparition of one Choriambic is hardly
sufficient evidence. The chief speakers appear to be a woman,
a maid, and a sea-captain who is in liquor. He uses nautical
language : ' you have been cruising about (περιπέπλευκας) with
some one else: my timbers are shivered ', κατέαγμαι· ἐρῶ,
μαίνομαι. Then apparently a sailor comes to say that the
boat is loaded, and there the fragment breaks off.

A similar fragment containing the outpourings of a drunken
lover was found on an Egyptian potsherd of about 100 B.C.[1]
Although this is mainly in prose, the chief speaker uses high-
flown poetical terms which he either invents or remembers,
appealing, for instance, to Ναΐδες ἀβρόσφυροι.

Παῖς ἀλεκτρυόνα ἀπολέσας [2] is the title given by Crusius to
a fragment belonging to the first part of the first century,
written in a rude and uncertain metre which Crönert calls
' Ionic Tetrametri effrenati ' : one recognizes Choriambics and
Paeons at the end of the lines. A boy is lamenting the loss of
a pet fighting-cock :

> χάριν τούτου ἐκαλούμην μέγας ἐν τῷ βίῳ,
> καὶ ἐλεγόμην μακάριος ἀνδράσιν τοῖς φιλοτρόφοις.
> ψυχορραγῶ.

' My cock has fallen in love with a hen, and has deserted me.'
The hen is called by a curious name θακαθαλπάς, which may
be an onomatopoeic word, but which Bechtel has altered,
probably rightly, to θακοθαλπάς, comparing Herondas vii. 48,
ὅκως νεοσσοὶ τὰς κοχώνας θάλποντες. The piece ends with
a pathetic farewell :

> ἀλλ' ἐπιθεὶς λίθον ἐματοῦ [3] ἐπὶ τὴν καρδίαν
> καθησυχάσομαι· ὑμεῖς δ' ὑγιαίνετε, φίλοι.

But there is one poem which takes us away from the hot
Alexandrian music-halls to the open air. The *Tebtunis
Papyri* [4] preserve a pretty poem in Anacreontic metre which
may possibly be earlier than the date of the Papyrus itself,
which is about A. D. 100. It describes a mountain glade, echo-

---

[1] Crusius, *Herondas*[5], p.137.   [2] Ib., p. 131.
[3] A vulgar form of ἐμαυτοῦ.   [4] *Tebtunis Papyri*, i, p. 3.

ing with the songs of birds, and full of busy bees which are described elaborately in a long string of epithets like that in the lines on the dolphins in the pseud-Arion.[1] The accumulated epithets are not used idly, but with knowledge and observation. The meaning, for instance, of πιθαναί and δυσέρωτες is not apparent at first sight; πιθαναί does not mean 'charming', as Dr. Schubart would have it, but recalls, with ἐργάτιδες following it, Shakespeare's

Endeavour . . .
To which is fixed, as an aim or butt,
Obedience, for so work the honey-bees,[2]

and δυσέρωτες is a bold and effective way of describing concisely the sexless worker-bee, for the description of which Virgil takes a line and a half.[3] The writer knew, too, of the mason-bee (apparently the only ancient writer who does), for one of his epithets is πηλουργοί. The scenery is not Egyptian; perhaps it may be a dell among the Sicilian mountains.

The *Berlin Papyri*[4] include a strange fragment in Anapaests, the first part of which contains a turgid eulogy of Homer. It opens with an enumeration of the various members of the Greek stock which honoured Homer as the founder of Heroic poetry. The following lines give an idea of the style:

τήν τ' ἀπὸ Μουσῶν ἄφθιτον αὐδήν,
ἣν σὺ μερίμναις ταῖσιν ἀτρύτοις
καθυφηνάμενος, πόντος τις ὅπως,
ἔπτυσας ἄλλοις . . .

The second part contains a sombre lament of Cassandra over Hecuba and herself, in which she intends to expound the meaning of the ancient oracles:

[και]ρὸς ἀνοίγειν [τὸν ὑ]πὸ σκοτίαις
βύβλοισι λόγον κρυπτόν· ἀνάγκη
πρὸς φῶς μ' ἆ[σαι].

One naturally thinks of Lycophron's Alexandra as a parallel to this part. The crabbed and artificial style points to a Hellenistic date, perhaps to the first part of the second century B. C.

---

[1] [Arion], 7, 8.   [2] *Henry V*, i. 2.
[3] Virg. *Georg*. iv. 198, 199.   [4] *Berlin. Klass. Texte*, v. 2, p. 131.

The final extract from the Berlin collection brings us back
to an earlier age and a kind of classical poetry of which we
have too few examples, the Scolia, short songs or ballads for
social gatherings. A Papyrus [1] containing a number of short
poems was found in Egypt, at Elephantine, in the grave of
a Greek mercenary soldier, and had clearly been buried with
him. The soldier had written down in his own handwriting,
which cannot be later than 300 B. C., the words of some
favourite ballads, no doubt for his own use at some merry-
making of his messmates. There are six altogether, and the
titles of some are given in the margin, Μοῦσαι, Εὐφωρατ[ίς]
(probably), Μνημοσύνη. Μοῦσαι is a mere fragment, but
Εὐφωρατίς is complete. The title means 'The Scout's Goddess': 'Pulcra Laverna speculatorum', as the Berlin editors
happily render it ; either in the sense of prospering or detect-
ing the scout. It contains a brief account of the fate of Dolon :
'into our songs we will weave the tale of her who cut down
the spy.'

Μνημοσύνη, which is not quite perfectly preserved, describes
in rather dithyrambic language a ship being caught in a squall,
and the orders shouted to the sailors as she runs for safety.
The metre of both these ballads is Dactylo-epitrite.

A poem of ten complete elegiacs forms a kind of epilogue to
the collection. It is the address of a Symposiarch, called
here ὁ ποταρχῶν (a new word), to the party, reminding them
of the three parts of their duty : of taking their share in the
merriment, of listening to one another, and of obeying the
chair :

ἥδ' ἀρετὴ συμποσίου πέλεται.

Note.

Two lyric poems in the *Oxyrhynchus Papyri* and one in the
Berlin. Klassikertexte, although of some interest, belong to
a later period. The first two are of some importance in the
history of Greek metre, for they are probably to be scanned
partly by quantity and partly by accent. The first (*Oxyrhynchus Papyri*, vol. iii, No. 425) is in the Anapaestic metre with

[1] *Berlin. Klass. Texte*, v. 2, p. 56.

a fourth Paeon in the last foot. Sailors are called upon to sing the comparison (Σύγκρισις) of nautical life on the Nile and at sea. Such Συγκρίσεις were common in Imperial times.

The second (*Oxyrh. Pap.* xi, No. 1383) is entitled 'Ροδίοις ἀνέμοις, and is an appeal to the winds and waves by some one who is weather-bound, that they may fall. The accentual scansion is more marked in this poem than in the first. The last is a Lyric poem to Fortune, (*Berlin. Klass. Texte*, v. 2, 142), and consists of the commonplace description of Fortune who raises the lowly and brings down the proud. The metre is uncertain, a Dactylic and Iambic medley, and the poem belongs to the time when the lines of the classical lyric structure had been forgotten.   J. U. P.

(iii) *The Nome.*

The Persae of Timotheus.

The Papyrus, which contains more than 250 lines of the Citharoedic Nomos of Timotheus, entitled Πέρσαι, ' has the distinction ', says Sir F. Kenyon,[1] ' of being the oldest Greek literary manuscript in existence, dating from the end of the fourth century B.C.' It was discovered in 1902 in a grave near Abusir in Egypt, and edited with a Greek paraphrase and a commentary by Wilamowitz-Moellendorff in the following year. It is now in the Berlin Museum.

Three lines were already known to us, including the opening line

Κλεινὸν ἐλευθερίας τεύχων μέγαν Ἑλλάδι κόσμον
(Bergk, *P. L. G.*[4], Fr. 8, 9, 10),

and

σέβεσθ' αἰδῶ συνεργὸν ἀρετᾶς δοριμάχου,

both in a grandiose style.

An incident is told by Plutarch which illustrates the popularity [2] of the piece, a century after its first production.

---

[1] *Quarterly Review*, ccviii, p. 336.
[2] Plut. *Philopoemen*, ch. xi.

At the Nemean games of 207/6, Philopoemen, shortly after his victory over the Spartans at Mantinea, entered with the officers of his staff into the theatre while the musical competitions were being held, and when the musician Pylades had just begun to sing the *Persae* with a voice well suited to the lofty style (ὄγκος) of the poetry. The whole audience, at the first line,[1] turned their gaze upon Philopoemen, and broke into joyous applause, while the hope of reviving the ancient glories of Greece reanimated their hearts, and awoke a gleam of their proud spirit of old.

In the *Persae* of Timotheus we possess an example of Greek Melic poetry popularized, and degraded in the process. Before the discovery of this Papyrus, there were indications in ancient literature that at the end of the fifth century B. C. all was not well with musical poetry. There are the well-known passages in the *Laws* and the *Republic*, wherein Plato complains of a spirit of innovation. The old-fashioned categories of Melic composition were disappearing ; the division of this branch of poetry into the monodic and the choral, and the subdivisions in either branch according as the accompanying instrument was the αὐλός or the κιθάρα, and the further subdivisions which depended upon the person addressed, the place, and the position or motions of the singers. Now were being produced works which were neither Nomes nor Dithyrambs, neither θρῆνοι nor ὕμνοι, but something between the two. And with this relaxation of structure went a corresponding relaxation of all the laws of musical sobriety. There were new modes, new ἁρμονίαι, wild and plaintive and sensuous beyond the bounds of decorum. And the cause of all this Plato finds, as might be expected, in a pursuit of ἡδονὴ μᾶλλον τοῦ δέοντος.[2]

There are echoes of these complaints in contemporary and later literature, and Timotheus is often mentioned as the worst offender. Aristophanes, although he disliked the ‘new music’, does not attack him, partly perhaps because his time was fully occupied with Euripides ; but there is extant a fragment

---

[1] Quoted above.   [2] *Rep.* 411 A ; *Laws* 700 E.

of Pherecrates[1] or Nicomachus complaining of the extrava-
gance of his diction and his tunes, a fragment which would
carry more weight if its own diction were not so extravagant.
Antiphanes[2] makes mention of the extraordinary metaphor
by which he called a shield φιάλην Ἄρεως, ' the cup of Ares '.
And later there is the matter-of-fact Suidas, who sums up the
indictment in general terms, τὴν ἀρχαίαν μουσικὴν ἐπὶ τὸ
μαλακώτερον μετήγαγεν.

From Plutarch and Suidas can be gathered indications of
certain steps in this development or decadence. Terpander,
the father of the Nome, who lived in Lesbos about 700 B. C.,
had but seven strings to his lyre, but by the end of the fifth
century the number had been increased to eleven.[3] Whether
the names and numbers are correct or not, this shows that the
music became more and more elaborate. At the same time
it grew imitative rather than expressive. This is probably
pointed to by the νιγλάρους of ' Pherecrates ',[4] for if in your
poem you mentioned a whistling wind, you made the music
whistle. We also find that it was probably Melanippides[5] who
broke down the structure of the older style by first writing
Dithyrambs in a ' free' rhythm, that is, a rhythm neither
monostrophic, such as a series of hexameters, nor triadic, i. e.
consisting of Strophe, Antistrophe, and Epode. Finally, when
Dithyramb had displaced all other forms of Melic except the
Nome, and had become wild and extravagant, it reacted upon
the Nome, causing it to share its own corruption.

So we find a process extending through a series of more or
less well-known names and culminating in that of Timotheus ;[6]
a process marked by the elaboration of the music, the liberation

---

[1] Pherecr., Fr. 145 K.   [2] Fr. 112 K.

[3] The names of the composers and the number of strings which they use
is uncertain. Timotheus (*Pers.* 242) speaks of his ῥυθμοὶ ἑνδεκακρούματοι:
Ion (of Chios?), Fr. 3, Bergk, *P. L. G.*⁴, has ἑνδεκάχορδε λύρα: Pherecrates, 145 K, ll. 5 and 25, attributes χορδαὶ δώδεκα both to Melanippides
and Timotheus. See *Lyra* in Daremberg-Saglio, and Wilamowitz's
edition of the *Persae*, p. 75.

[4] Pherecr., Fr. 145 K, l. 26.   [5] Ib., l. 4.

[6] The statement in Clem. Alex. *Strom.* i, ch. xvi. 79, that Timotheus
combined chorus and harp in Nomes, and that in Plut. *de Mus.* 1132 E,
are not free from difficulty. If he did so, this particular contamination
of the Nome with the Dithyramb completed its corruption.

of the rhythm from the prescribed forms, and the expansion
of the bounds of permissibility in the choice of the subject.
This process is thought by most of the judges of antiquity to
be one of decadence rather than of development, though occasionally a half-hearted note of praise is sounded. Thus even
Plato admits (*Legg.* 700 E) that the musicians of the new
school are φύσει μὲν ποιητικοί, though dull in their apprehension of good taste, and Plutarch in one passage calls the music
of Timotheus φιλάνθρωπος.[1] Aristotle apparently [2] treats him
as a person whose work can be quoted by persons of culture, and
has no objection even to the notorious φιάλην Ἄρεως, probably
because it admirably adapts itself to his mathematical but
uninspired treatment of metaphor.[3] But more noteworthy
than this is the story preserved by Plutarch that Timotheus at
first found no success, but was encouraged by no less a person
than Euripides, who told him that he would 'soon have the
audiences at his feet'[4] Satyrus indeed records that Euripides
wrote the prologue to the *Persae*,[5] which unfortunately has not
survived. This is not the place to inquire how far Euripides
himself shows traces of 'decadence' in the lyrics of his later
tragedies. But the approbation of the tragedian can surely
be set against the censure of Pherecrates. And finally there
is the fact that Timotheus did eventually meet with the success
predicted for him. We are told that the Ephesians gave him
1,000 pieces of gold for his *Artemis*,[6] and he ended by
gaining a place in the highest literary circles of his time.

But still the judgement of Philosophy and the Old Comedy
carried the day, and while yet no considerable literary fragment of the later Melic was extant, critics were quite prepared
to say how bad it was.[7] Timotheus himself could only be

[1] He couples him with Philoxenus, τὸν φιλάνθρωπον καὶ θεματικὸν ('calculated for effect') νῦν ὀνομαζόμενον τρόπον διώξαντες (*de Musica*, 1135 D).
[2] *Poet.* ii.   [3] *Poet.* xxi. 12.
[4] Plut. *An Seni Resp.* 795 D ὡς ὀλίγου χρόνου τῶν θεάτρων ὑπ' αὐτῷ γενησομένων.
[5] Satyrus in *Oxyrh. Pap.* ix, col. xxii. For a discussion of this see the section on Satyrus.
[6] Alexander Aetolus, ap. Macrob. *Sat.* v. 21.
[7] e.g. Müller: 'a loose and wanton play of lyrical sentiments, redundant and luxurious.'

judged by a few very short fragments, one of course the extraordinary φιάλην Ἄρεως, another the no less imaginative (μίξας) αἷμα Βακχίου νεορρύτοις δακρύοισι Νυμφᾶν, that is, wine and water.[1] But when a considerable fragment of the *Persae* was discovered at Oxyrhynchus, it seemed as if the last word could now be said, and the criticisms of antiquity were justified to the hilt.

The *Persae* is a 'Nome'. A 'Nome' was originally a slow and stately composition, sung by a single voice to the accompaniment of the κιθάρα, and having for its subject 'the majesty and benevolence of the gods', or 'a prayer for the prosperity of the worshippers' (Weir Smyth, *Melic Poets*, Introd.). Its appropriate metre was the hexameter, or some other form of a stateliness corresponding to the subject. But very little of this survives in the *Persae*. It is true that it was sung to the κιθάρα, and was monodic, though possibly chorally monodic (that is, the chorus all sang together as one individual). But the metre is the freest of the free. It moves along in short and simple phrases which have a lilt of their own, but no more dignity than a nursery rhyme. The subject is the battle of Salamis, and is treated entirely, if not with a view to comic effect, yet with a view to getting as much banging and splashing as possible out of that event.[2] There are crashes of ramming ships, blows with oars and cudgels, flights and shrieks of terror, puffings and splutterings of drowning men, who gasp out curses as they struggle. And the diction is monstrous. There is a profusion of unwieldy metaphor. Oars are χεῖρες ἐλάτιναι : short sticks are ἀποτομάδες βουδόροι (that is, 'cuttings such as men use to beat oxen') : the throat is the τρόφιμον ἄγγος: teeth are μαρμαροφεγγεῖς παῖδες στόματος, or, less ornately, γόμφοι. Along with metaphor epithet runs riot. The sea is described by ἰχθυστεφέσι μαρμαροπτέροις κόλποισιν Ἀμφιτρίτας, or some 'strong swimmer

---

[1] Fr. 7 Wilam.

[2] He had described a storm in his *Nauplius* (if the title is correct), but not successfully, as his critic thinks. Hegesandros ap. Athen. viii. 338 A Δωρίων καταγελῶν τοῦ ἐν τῷ Τιμοθέου Ναυπλίῳ (ναυτίλῳ A corr. Casaub.) χειμῶνος ἔφασκεν ἐν κακκάβᾳ ζεούσᾳ μείζονα ἑωρακέναι χειμῶνα. Wilam. Tim. Fr. 10.

in his agony' addresses it as οἰστρομανὲς παλεομίσημ' ἄπιστόν τ' ἀγκάλισμα κλυσιδρομάδος αὔρας. And there is the double compound, which is a sure sign of decadence. For instance, λευκός means 'white', and λευκόπτερος means first 'white-winged' and secondarily simply 'white', as it is often found in tragedy. The next step is to tack on another substantive, and evolve some such word as (let us say) λευκοπτερόθριξ to mean 'white-haired'. Thus Timotheus presents us with μακραυχενόπλους of the 'long-voyaging' oar, and μελαμπεταλοχίτωνα as an epithet of the knees of Cybele.

The only admirer of such a style can be the philologist; for we are bound to recognize the philological value of the author in illustrating the flexibility and fecundity of the Greek language. All Greek poetry shows this amazing creativeness in formation, and not least that recently discovered in Papyri. The same power which produced the pictorial epithets of Bacchylides and the whimsical compounds of Cercidas appears in the extravagant facility of Timotheus. But not content with his achievements in the Greek language, he breaks out in one passage into a string of barbaric utterances in broken Greek, when a captured Asiatic, dragged along by his hair by a σιδαρόκωπος Ἑλλάν, 'breaks the seal of his lips with a piercing shriek in his quest of the Ionian tongue'! (162 ff.) and produces the monstrosities ἦξε, ἔρχω, κάθω, and Ἄρτιμις, ἐμὸς μέγας θεός.

Yet in this welter of bad taste there are one or two extenuating circumstances. It is perhaps as unfair to judge Timotheus by his bare language as to judge an Oratorio by the words alone. It must be remembered that he represents the consummation of a process which had as its object the subordination of the words to the music. And when the music is imitative rather than expressive, the words must of necessity follow it. This process was bound to meet the opposition of the conservative school and the champions of σωφροσύνη. But it would be a hard matter to prove that the object was in itself illegitimate, and indeed highly unfair to attempt this without such a knowledge of the music itself as we are unlikely ever to possess. The innovations for which Timotheus was

ARGH

responsible were deliberate. His aim was entirely different
from that of the old school. He cannot bear the monotony
of the μουσοπαλαιολύμας, λωβητῆρας ἀοιδᾶν, κηρύκων λιγυμα-
κροφώνων τείνοντας ἰυγάς (229), the declamatory hexameters
and simple modes of the ancient Nome. He is proud of his
eleven-stringed lyre. οὐκ ἀείδω τὰ παλαιά,[1] says he. In the
Persae he is trying to give a musical impression of a sea-fight,
according to the new style, which is as far removed from
Aeschylus as Aeschylus is from Homer. His object as a
champion of popular realism is to present a sea-fight as it
really is: and it is not a solemn conflict of souls predestined
to victory or a glorious death, or at least not till after the
event: it is a vortex of strange and unearthly pantings and
gaspings and blows and splashes and curses, with an under-
current of deadly endeavour ; and no words of the poet can be
wilder than the reality. Of course it has been asserted time
after time that this realism is not art at all : and this is not the
place to fight the battle once more. But at all events we must
acquit Timotheus of the charge of being so destitute of taste
as to imagine that his poem, when *read* in cold blood, could
produce the effect for which he was striving. It was not
meant to be read, but to be sung ; and words and metre had to
be chosen which would adapt themselves to that impression of
the event which the music was meant to convey.[2]   C. J. E.

[1] Weir Smyth, *Greek Melic Poets*, Tim. Fr. 7.
[2] For a vivid and brilliant account of the many faults of this astonishing
composition, see Professor Gilbert Murray's criticism in the preface to the
third edition of his *Ancient Greek Literature.* Sir F. Kenyon writes in
Greek Papyri, and their contribution to Classical Literature (Cambridge :
printed at the University Press, 1918), p. 7 : 'It is only by remembering
that his verses are but the libretto to a musical composition that we can
understand his being tolerated at all.' The rest of his criticism is as
severe as Professor Murray's.

III

COMEDY

Menander and other new Fragments of the New Comedy.

THE opening years of the twentieth century gave to the world a considerable portion of the work of one of the most interesting figures in the wide range of Greek literature, Menander, the Athenian, master of the New Comedy. He had already been known as the author of more than one hundred plays, but these had been so scantily remembered that it was impossible for scholars to judge how much truth there was in the famous words which were generally quoted whenever he was mentioned.[1] Many associated his name with collections of proverbial lines like those ascribed to Publilius Syrus in Roman literature. What the completed product of his art could be, none could say with certainty, but the judgement of Caesar the Dictator, Quintilian, and other competent critics, promised a literary treasure if fortune were willing.

The discoveries at Oxyrhynchus in Egypt had encouraged the hope that one more secret might be wrung from the grasp of her Sphinx, the secret of the New Comedy. A few fragments were rescued in the haunts of the dead, which threw more light on Menander. At last, in 1905, Lefebvre found in ancient Aphroditopolis the remains of no fewer than five of Menander's comedies, from which it is possible to arrive at some judgement on the work he did. Yet once again the niggard goddess has denied us her fullest favours. No play exists in such a form that scholars are unanimous as to the course its action took. Reconstruction is perilous. Literary fragments are not like human bones, one of which was sufficient for an Agassiz to reconstruct the whole body with tolerable certainty. Even single lines, when imperfect, cannot be restored with universal satisfaction, and later discoveries

---

[1]
$$\text{᾿Ω Μέναν δρε καὶ βίε,}$$
$$\text{πότερος ἄρ' ὑμῶν πότερον ἀπεμιμήσατο ;}$$
(by Aristophanes of Byzantium).

have shown that the most attractive suggestions may be wrong, or at least not quite correct. It is wisdom, however, to be content with what we have, remembering that ' the glorious gifts of the gods are not to be cast away '.[1]

The first fragment contains the opening scene of the "Ηρως (the Demigod), already known from quotations preserved by Stobaeus, Athenaeus, and others. It is particularly valuable, since a metrical Argument is prefixed to the play. We have, therefore, a document which presents in outline the whole scheme of one of the New Comedies. A list of nine characters contains the name of Hero, after whom the play is named ; his part may have corresponded with that of Ignorance in the Περικειρομένη.

The play itself opens with a dialogue between two slaves— Geta, a wood-cutter,[2] and Davus, a member of the household of Laches. The scene is some country district.[3] The two meet not far from the house in which Davus lives, perhaps on an occasion when Geta brought wood from the fields to the town. In an amusing scene Davus confesses he has fallen in love with some one in his own station of life.[4] To Geta's question whether she is a slave Davus replies by telling him her history. Tibeius, a freedman, was the reputed father of twins, Plango, the girl whom he loves, and Gorgias, the shepherd-boy. In his old age hard times compelled him to borrow two minae from Laches to support the children. When death took him Gorgias buried him with the few shillings he could scrape together, then passed into Laches' house together with his sister as security till the debt could be cleared off. Davus, brought into frequent contact with the girl, fell in love with her, and spoke to his master about it. The latter promised her in marriage, if he could get her brother's consent, and then was summoned to Lemnos on urgent business.

The main fragment ends at this point. From two others we learn that the twins are about eighteen years old, and that their

[1] References are made to A. Körte's Editio Maior in the Teubner text, 1912.
[2] l. 52.   [3] l. 45.
[4] l. 20. The mention of the influence of Τύχη is a feature of Menander's work. See below.

mother's name was Myrrhina. In a dialogue between
Myrrhina and her husband Laches, the subject of which is the
birth of the children, the mention of a Thracian woman[1] may
supply a clue to the plot. The outline in the argument is as
follows: ' Plangon had been seduced by a neighbour. Davus
took the blame upon himself. Myrrhina, Plangon's mother,
was upset when she heard about it. The truth then came
out. The father recognized his children, while Plangon's lover
married her.'

Reconstruction cannot but be conjectural. It is clear that
Davus's confession of his affection has taken place some three
months[2] before the action of the play begins, and some such
time must be allowed for the discovery of the intrigue. The
demi-god Hero may be some sort of abstract symbol express-
ing the interest the departed take in those they have left.
He may perhaps be an impersonation of the dead spirit of
Tibeius, who alone could know the true facts about the twins.
The Thracian servant[1] may have filled a rôle like that of the
Samian or of Sophrona in the 'Επιτρέποντες, taking Myrrhina's
children and giving them to Tibeius, together with some
trinkets or tokens which would establish their identity. This
receives strong support from the last line of the play, in which
Laches mentions a shepherd,[3] who can only have been Tibeius.
The method of recognition cannot be determined, as no hint
of the circumstantial evidence appears in the fragments.

The only character in the piece as it is preserved is Davus.
As a rule Davus is a cunning pander to some wild youth. He
is here quite a different character, actuated by the high
motive of self-sacrifice to save the reputation of one he loves.
He is evidently valued by his master, otherwise he would not
have obtained his ready consent to matrimony ; he as evidently
loves his master, whom he blesses, wishing him prosperity in
his voyage.[4]

It is clear then that set names in the New Comedy do not
always connote fixed types of character.

[1] l. 78. [2] l. 45 τρίμηνον, conjectural, but very probable.
[3] l. 83 ἐπ' ἐμαυτὸν ἔλαβον ποιμέν'.
[4] l. 46 σώζοιτο. l. 47 ὄνησις εἴη.

The next fragments are of great interest. They contain about 600 lines of the 'Ἐπιτρέποντες (the Guardians). This play had attracted the attention of Quintilian,[1] and was in the hands of Sidonius[2] at the end of the fifth century of our era. It opens with great spirit. Two slaves, Davus and Syriscus, are quarrelling. They agree to submit their case to the first citizen they meet. The choice falls upon Smicrines. He readily agrees to adjudicate, exacting a promise that they will abide by his decision. He then calls upon Davus, the less talkative, to state his case.

Davus tells him he was tending his sheep a month back, when he found a child with some trinkets about its neck and other ornaments. He took it home intending to rear it, but second thoughts made him alter his mind ; a child would bring anxiety and expense which he could not face.[3] Next morning Syriscus, a charcoal-burner, met him and begged him to let him have the child in place of one of his own who had died. Davus consented, much to Syriscus's joy, who heaped blessings on his head for his kindness. Later, however, he heard about the jewels, and on that very day came with his wife (who is a mute spectator of the scene) to demand the restoration of them. Davus refused, arguing that if Syriscus is not content with what he has already, all he need do is give back the child; but he himself should have some reward for his discovery.

Syriscus now states his case. Davus had deliberately concealed the existence of the jewels; it was only by a mere accident that he, Syriscus, knew of them. He claims that the infant boy himself is in court demanding their return, at the

---

[1] x. 1. 70.

[2] Sidon. *Ep.* iv. 12 'Nuper ego filiusque communis Terentianae Hecyrae sales ruminabamus; . . . quoque absolutius rhythmos comicos . . . sequeretur, ipse etiam fabulam similis argumenti, id est Epitrepontem [*sic* MSS.] Menandri, in manibus habebam.'

[3] MS. ll. 38-9   τί φροντίδων ἐμοὶ
                        τοιουτοσιτισην.

Edd. read τοιουτοσί τις ὤν (or ἦν), which does not make much sense. We should perhaps read τοιοῦτο σιτίζειν = 'why should I bother feeding it?' The corruption is due to the interchange of σ and ζ; comp. Περικειρ. l. 51 σώσατε or σῴζετε ; the MSS. differ.

same time dramatically holding him out towards Smicrines. To the question why he did not demand the trinkets at once, Syriscus replies that he was not then entitled to do so.[1] Again, the child is obviously born of well-to-do parents. If he grows to manhood in a slave's house, he might turn out to be a king, like one of the heroes in the Tragedies. Davus, therefore, has no right to rob the child of tokens that might prove his salvation. In fact, prudence is never amiss in a life which is full of pitfalls.[2] Davus's argument that Syriscus can return the child if he is not content is bad ; he would simply use him to play the villain with greater security.[3]

Smicrines then gives judgement. The articles belong to the child. Davus reluctantly hands them over, and Syriscus counts them out one by one into the folds of his wife's dress. As they are admiring them, Onesimus, the servant of Charisius, son of Chaerestratus, comes out of the house and at once recognizes a ring which his master lost at a revel. He takes it from Syriscus, who vainly protests that it belongs to the child. Onesimus promises to show it to his master on the morrow, and Syriscus agrees to wait as long in the city, reflecting that he has not done badly out of the case after all.

In the next scene Onesimus comes out of the house to report his failure to find an opportune moment for restoring the ring. Pamphila, Charisius's wife and Smicrines' daughter, had borne a child, probably while Charisius was away from home, within five months of her marriage. Onesimus had told his master, who had accordingly quarrelled with Pamphila, and taken up with a flute-girl, Habrotonon. Yet he was not grateful to his

---

[1] ll. 96–8.

[2] ll. 126–8

> ὄντ' ἐπισφαλῆ φύσει
> τὸν βίον ἁπάντων τῇ προνοίᾳ δεῖ, πάτερ,
> τηρεῖν, πρὸ πολλῶν ταῦθ' ὁρῶντ' ἐξ ὧν ἔνι.

This passage alone entitles its author to a place among the classics.

[3] ll. 131–4

> οὐκ ἔστι δίκαιον εἴ τι τῶν τούτου σὲ δεῖ
> ἀποδιδόναι, καὶ τοῦτο πρὸς ζητεῖς λαβεῖν,
> ἵν' ἀσφαλέστερον πονηρεύσῃ πάλιν
> εἰ νῦν τι τῶν τούτου σέσωκεν ἡ Τύχη.

We should perhaps simply read οὐκ ἐπὶ δικαίων, στ supplanting π, as often in MSS. = 'If you are forced to give up anything of the child's, you cannot on any just plea (comp. ἐπ' ἴσης, L. & S. ἴσος, iv. 2) try to keep as well anything which Chance has saved, to be more secure in your villainies.' τοῦτο is the antecedent to εἴ τι, which = ὅ.

servant for ruining his domestic happiness. Onesimus is in the act of regretting his having betrayed his mistress, when Habrotonon is forcibly ejected from the house, Charisius no longer finding any pleasure in her society. Filled with a pity for his wasteful life, she turns to mourn her own lot. At that moment Syriscus appears, looking for Onesimus. He sees him [1] and demands the ring. Onesimus tells him how the ring was lost at the Tauropolia, when Charisius probably corrupted some young girl who was compelled to expose their child. Syriscus is not quite convinced, but promises to return to see what can be done in the matter. As Onesimus is considering what he should do, Habrotonon, approaching him, learns the situation, and adds her story. She says she was present at the Tauropolia on that very occasion. A handsome young girl who had been outraged ran up with her clothes torn, one whom she would recognize at once if she saw her again. The ring itself would prove nothing ; Charisius might have lost it at dice or given it as a pledge ; but the ring *and* the child would be overwhelming evidence. She suggests therefore that she should go in herself with the child, impersonating the girl. If Charisius turned out to be the father, the mother could no doubt easily be found. Taking the ring, she walks boldly into the house, uttering a prayer to Persuasion, for her aim is her freedom. Onesimus, after contrasting her cunning with his heavier wit, prophesying that he will be ' a servant still ', bitterly repents the unwisdom of his too ready tongue and the loss of his master's favour. Seeing the approach of Smicrines, he leaves the stage.

Another lacuna occurs at this point. It is clear that Smicrines enters into conversation with a cook, who probably tells him about Charisius's amour with the flute-girl and his ill treatment of his wife, Smicrines' daughter. Later, Smicrines and Charisius evidently have a violent quarrel, the former going in to console his daughter, the latter to see the end, a happier one, as it proved, than he could ever have dreamed.

---

[1] l. 226 οὗτος ἔνδον ὠγαθέ. The line is faulty : a trochee, or its equivalent, is missing. Edd. insert ἀπόδος after ἔνδον, but the latter word is corrupt. May we read οὗτος, ἦν ἰδού· δὸς ὠγαθέ? ἦν appears in *Samia*, l. 98 ; ἰδού ib. l. 97. δός may have disappeared after ἰδού by haplography.

In the next act Habrotonon is discovered with the child. Pamphila, after her interview with her father, comes out praying some god to have pity on her. Habrotonon, at once recognizing her, tells her that the child is hers: she reminds her of the Tauropolia, admitting that she pretended to be the mother till the real mother appeared. Pointing out that Heaven *has* pitied her, she accepts her invitation to go inside and tell the whole story. Onesimus now comes out describing the result of the interview between Smicrines and his daughter. Charisius overheard it; his wife's loyalty to him and her defence of his actions filled him with mingled feelings of self-reproach and regret for the ruin of what might have been a happy wedded life. So great was the effect on his mind, that Onesimus dreaded loss of his reason and his own punishment. Charisius himself comes out and makes his recantation in a speech which is unhappily incomplete.[1]

The connexion of the fragments at this point is highly questionable. It appears that Habrotonon informs Charisius that the child is his wife's, filling him with joy, while (probably in the next act) Chaerestratus, Charisius's father, appears on the stage to share in the good news, recommending liberty as Habrotonon's reward for her faithfulness, cleverness, and zeal.

Nothing now remains but to acquaint Smicrines with the happy turn which events have taken. He comes on to the stage in violent altercation with Sophrona, Pamphila's nurse, who tries to dissuade him from recovering his daughter and her dowry from her husband. Beating violently on the door, he is treated by Onesimus to a lecture on Divine Providence[2] which is vital for an understanding of Menander's art. The servant solemnly recommends him to live a less passionate

---

[1] Pamphila, defending her husband, pleaded (ll. 499-501) that she

κοινωνὸς ἥκειν τοῦ βίου
παρ' ἄνδρα, κοὐ δεῖν τἀτύχημ' αὐτὴν φυγεῖν
τὸ συμβεβηκός.

φυγεῖν can bear only a very forced meaning, 'evade the duty of facing'. It misses the whole point of her defence. The right reading is possibly ψέγειν, 'criticize'.

[2] ll. 547-68.

life and in future to keep a warier eye on a marriageable girl—
this because he is lucky enough to be the first to tell him of
the birth of a grandson. He informs him too that Sophrona
knows a good deal about the Tauropolia and the child. To
an incredulous question from Smicrines she answers with great
self-complacency [1] and with a singularly happy quotation from
Euripides, naming the play (the *Auge*), and offering to quote
the whole speech. So the fragments bid them farewell, and
we wish them true happiness.

This outline may perhaps convey some idea of the skill with
which the master wove his plots; but nothing can give any
adequate impression of the zest with which he wrote except
a perusal of the text itself. It captivates us because it cipti-
vated Menander first, just as Henry IV carries us away
because it intoxicated Shakespeare with the joy of pure
creation. The action never flags: the characters live and
energize the story; the minor personages are individualized,
each receiving the personal touch which makes him an independent living soul. Throughout the play this characteriza-
tion is effected by a most skilful juxtaposition and contrast.
Davus is dour and reticent; [2] Syriscus is keen, voluble, and
wide awake. Of the subordinate characters he is the best gift
that the fragments have bestowed upon us: he is quite
irresistible.

Onesimus and Habrotonon are similarly contrasted; they
are valuable as a study of the different forms which cunning
self-interest would take in a slave. Both long for liberty, [3] but
the woman's readier wit and imagination immediately discern
the way to the end even when her chances seem to be ruined. [4]
She plays her cards with calm confidence: aided by an excellent memory, [5] skilful acting, [6] courage, [7] and the useful art of

---

[1] l. 587 παθαινομένη.   [2] l. 22 ὁ σιωπῶν.   [3] ll. 331 and 343.

[4] ll. 340-3   τοπαστικὸν τὸ γύναιον, ὡς ἥσθηθ' ὅτι
κατὰ τὸν ἔρωτ' οὐκ ἔστ' ἐλευθερίας τυχεῖν
ἄλλως δ' ἀλύει, τὴν ἑτέραν πορεύεται
ὁδόν.

[5] l. 267.

[6] ll. 309-10   τὰ κοινὰ ταυτὶ δ' ἀκκιοῦμαι τῷ λόγῳ
τοῦ μὴ διαμαρτεῖν.

[7] ll. 437-51.

echoing another's sentiments,[1] she wins a high compliment
from Chaerestratus as well as her liberty.[2] May the gods send
her a good man who is in search of a thrifty housewife.[3]

Onesimus has a difficult problem before him. He has
forfeited his master's favour by his slanders, and rues his
indiscretion.[4] He dreads a second interview,[5] whereas
Habrotonon boldly enters even after she has been forcibly
ejected. He is in a complete quandary;[6] his intelligence is
judged by his desire to go in with the ring but without the
child, whereas the flute-girl points out that both are necessary
for a cogent proof.[7] His personality is completely dominated
by hers, and he can hope for freedom only through her success.[8]
When he claims from her a share in her certain reward she
retorts with ironical courtesy that she will always acknowledge
his part in her good luck.[9] Such a nature as his cannot rise
much above suspecting others of its own cunning, threatening
dire consequences if it is worsted.[10] When the good news is
confirmed, he can hope for his freedom only by an impertinent
attempt to goad Smicrines to fury, trusting to the excessive
joy a thoroughly angry nature might reasonably be expected
to feel. Like Malvolio, his tongue can 'tang arguments' of
Providence, which he can utter ' by great swarths ', but the best
criticism of his character is passed on him by his own self[11]
While Habrotonon's cunning is creative, because it is intelligent, Onesimus's is merely adaptive, because it lacks foresight.
We feel sure he is right; he will be ' a servant still ', and
deserves to be.[12]

---

[1] Pamphila (l. 434) prays Heaven to pity her: Habrotonon points to the
answer to her prayer, l. 453.

[2] ll. 514-15   οὐ γάρ ἐστ' ἄφρον
ἑταιρίδιον τοῦτ', οὐδὲ τὸ τυχὸν ἐπλάσατο.

[3] She pities Charisius's prodigality, l. 220:
τί τοσοῦτον ἀργύριον ἀπολλύει;

[4] ll. 205-6   τῶν πρότερόν μοι μεταμέλει
μηνυμάτων.

[5] ll. 231, 480.

[6] l. 275.

[7] ll. 316-17.

[8] ll. 322-5, 345-6.

[9] ll. 326-7.

[10] l. 334   ἂν γὰρ κακοηθεύσῃ, μαχοῦμαί σοι τότε.

[11] ll. 343-5   ἀλλ' ἐγὼ τὸν πάντα δουλεύσω χρόνον,
λέμφος, ἀπόπληκτος, οὐδαμῶς προνοητικὸς
τὰ τοιαῦτα.

[12] l. 346 καὶ γὰρ δίκαιον.

Smicrines is firmly drawn. His arbitration concerning the child is striking and final; it won Quintilian's praise,[1] and should win ours too. His obvious sense of what is just makes him all the more acutely indignant at his daughter's maltreatment. His interview with Charisius would have been a masterpiece had it survived. His daughter Pamphila appears but once, yet she is in every way worthy of her father. The same resolution in insisting on the fulfilment of a moral and legal obligation appears in the daughter; her place is at her husband's side, whom she sincerely loves in spite of his faults. Her high worth is attested by her husband [2] in contrast with his own unworthiness. We may be sure that happiness and concord will be re-established between them, cemented by the memory of their misunderstandings and by the presence of the child so wonderfully restored.

Of Charisius it is not easy to speak. The premature birth of a child destroyed his confidence in his young wife, but his liaison with the flute-girl was a mere act of bravado, with no affection behind it, rather hatred.[3] The loss of his wife's society plunged him into wild habits [4] and made him hate her betrayer.[5] When he discovers her unshaken loyalty to him, his return to himself is a stroke of genius which makes us love Menander for the inspiration which begat it. Glad as we are for the gift of the few fragments that remain, we cannot help feeling some resentment in being denied a full-length study of a character whose outlines are so attractive; it would have been one of the products of Menander's matured experience.

The next play has been provisionally entitled $\Sigma a\mu i a$ (the Samian Woman), since the name occurs twice in the fragment, applied to Chrysis, who plays an important part; and a single line [6] which contains it, and seems to suit the plot, has been preserved by Phrynichus.

---

[1] x. 1. 70; the text is uncertain, but the meaning clear.

[2] ll. 469-70
$$o\~iav \ \lambda a\beta \grave{\omega} v$$
$$\gamma vva\^i\chi' \ \acute{o} \ \mu \acute{\epsilon}\lambda \epsilon os \ \acute{\eta}\tau \acute{v}\chi \eta \kappa a.$$

[3] ll. 215-16
$$\grave{\epsilon}\rho \^a\sigma \theta ai \ \mu \grave{\epsilon}v \ \grave{\epsilon}\delta \acute{o}\kappa ovv$$
$$\theta \epsilon \^iov \ \delta \grave{\epsilon} \ \mu i\sigma \epsilon \^i \ \mu \^i\sigma os \ \acute{a}v\theta \rho \omega \pi \acute{o}s \ \mu \acute{\epsilon} \ \tau i.$$

[4] l. 305 $\mu \epsilon \theta \acute{v}\omega v$.   [5] ll. 481-2.   [6] Fr. 437 K.

The fragment begins with a soliloquy by Demeas, who is preparing the marriage feast of his son Moschio. The bride is Plango, the daughter of a neighbour Niceratus. Demeas had gone up into his store-chamber to get a few necessaries. A child was lying on a bed crying. Moschio's old nurse came downstairs, saw the child and soothed it, saying she had done the same for Moschio, its father. At that moment another servant came in, warning her that Demeas was somewhere about; the nurse slipped out quickly, regretting her words. But Demeas had heard everything. Coming out quickly he noticed Chrysis, the Samian woman, his mistress, suckling the child. The suspicion at once crossed his mind that his son had corrupted his paramour; unable, however, to reconcile such an idea with his son's willingness to marry Plango and his dutiful behaviour, he determined to make further inquiries before taking definite action.

At that moment Parmeno, a slave, appears to make the due preparations for the feast. Demeas asks him about the child. Parmeno at first pretends that it is the son of Chrysis and Demeas himself, but under threat of punishment he admits that the father is Moschio, and then takes refuge in flight. Convinced that his son has betrayed him, Demeas throws the blame on the woman, the Helen of his house.[1] He determines to save his son's reputation and cast the Samian on the streets. He rushes into the house, returning in a moment with her, and bids her begone, alleging as his reason her having taken up the child without his consent. Reminding her of her absolute poverty when she came to him, he tells her she did not know when she was well off, and warns her of her ultimate fate.

Chrysis is then left standing before the door of the house, weeping. Niceratus, coming out of his house, sees her there and asks about her trouble. Learning what has happened, he criticizes her for taking up the child, but is indignant with Demeas. Chrysis points out that there must be some other reason, as he was not angry when he first heard of it, only just before the marriage.

[1] l. 122 τὴν ἐμὴν Ἑλένην.

After a lacuna there follows one of the most amusing scenes in all the fragments. It is one of wild confusion.[1] It seems that Demeas has found out the truth about the child, and that Niceratus has guessed that the mother is his daughter. Fearful that the marriage will be broken off, he rushes into the house to get at the real facts. Chrysis, however, had persuaded Plango and her mother to deny everything. Niceratus intends to get hold of the child, even if he has to murder Chrysis, who rushes out with the baby, pursued by Niceratus. Demeas stops him, giving Chrysis time to get away safely into his own house. Niceratus turns on him, but Demeas assures him the marriage will take place, then invites him to take a turn or two with him in front of the house while they try to guess who is the father. Very gravely he reminds him how Zeus got through the roof of a house to visit Danae. As Niceratus admits that his roof leaks all over, Demeas has little hesitation in pronouncing Zeus to be the father. Not only so, but there are one or two of their acquaintance who can only be the sons of the gods; their lives declare it. This cogent proof completely satisfies them both, and the scene ends in the greatest harmony.

In the last act Moschio appears, indignant because of his father's suspicion. Were it not for his affection for the girl, he would have trailed the pike in Bactria or Caria. He is determined to frighten his father somehow. He catches sight of Parmeno, who has recovered from his fright and is ashamed of himself for having run away from an old man, although he had done nothing wrong. Moschio calls to him, and bids him fetch out a cloak and a sword. He comes back without them, but Moschio maltreats him, sending him in again. Meanwhile he reflects what will happen if his father really lets him go; he is sure to become a laughing-stock. The rest is lost.

[1] ll. 202-3, MS.   τὸ δεῖνα. μικρόν, ὦ τᾶν· οἴχομαι·
πάντα ταπραγματ' ἀνατέτραπται· τέλος ἔχει· νὴ τὸν Δία.
We should read πάντα ταράγματ'. The speaker evidently gasps out these disjointed sentences. ' By the way. One moment, sir. I'm done for. *All is mixed.* Topsy-turvy. All's over.' Comp. ll. 220-1 :
οὐδεπώποτ' ἐς τοσαύτην ἐμπεσών, μὰ τοὺς θεούς,
οἶδα ταραχήν.

It is not difficult to see how the play will end. The families
will be united, Chrysis being duly rewarded for her fidelity to
the young couple. The leading character in these fragments
is Demeas. He is not easily provoked,[1] weighs all the evidence
for and against a case,[2] and is above being duped.[3] His
standard of judgement is a person's character.[4] For his son's
sake he denies himself.[5] This is the explanation of his
reminding Chrysis of her poverty, language which is not more
painful to us than it must have been to him. A character
like this is not easily awed by mere noise and tumult. In
his firm and yet delicate hands Niceratus soon forgets his
passion, accepting without a murmur an explanation which is
in itself absurd, but sufficient for its purpose and the person
to whom it is offered. It would have been instructive to
see how he handles his son's somewhat transparent plan of
frightening him.

Chrysis is the next figure that attracts our attention. She
must have possessed some strong features to attract the notice
of a man like Demeas; this antecedent probability is borne
out by her actions. She is not afraid of him, even when he
thrusts her out; her speeches are calm, short, and to the
point.[6] She faces the world out of sheer loyalty to Demeas's
son and to Plango. Her best reward would be a place of
honour in the house to which circumstances so strangely
restored her.

Niceratus is a splendid success. He is poor, but he pro-
vides the sacrificial sheep which is necessary for his daughter's
marriage,[7] and on which he has probably spent the money
that should have mended his roof. He deserves the good
fortune which made his daughter desirable in the eyes of his
richer neighbour's son, and will no doubt continue to merit
the serious confidences of Demeas.

Moschio has evidently been well trained by his father, who
has noted his orderly and temperate behaviour.[8] Like other

---

[1] l. 56 οὐκ ἀγανακτῶν οὐδέπω.   [2] ll. 57–64.
[3] l. 100.   [4] l. 132 τὸν τρόπον δ' ὁρῶ.
[5] l. 135 ἐπιλαθοῦ τοῦ πόθου, πέπαυσ' ἐρῶν . . . διὰ τὸν υἱόν.
[6] ll. 154–75.   [7] ll. 184–7.   [8] l. 58 κοσμίω.

youths in Menander who have led young girls astray, he is
man enough to be true to his promise to love Plango,[1] heartily
desiring the marriage.[2] As years pass over him we are sure
that his father's deep influence will mould him to a goodly
manhood.

The Περικειρομένη (the Shorn Lady) was already known
from two fragments and from an epigram in the Anthology
(v. 217). The recently-discovered Papyri have preserved about
450 lines in a fairly complete form. The last 50 lines were
published in 1899 by Messrs. Grenfell and Hunt in vol. ii of
their Oxyrhynchus documents, No. 211; the greater portion
of the remainder is contained in the great 'Papyrus Cairensis',
which was discovered by Lefebvre in 1905 at Kôm-Ischkaou,
the ancient Aphroditopolis. Two other fragments, one at
Leipzig and the other at Heidelberg, are available for the
text; the latter adds nothing to Lefebvre's documents, but
the former contributes 73 lines not otherwise known.

The play as we have it opens with a remarkable prologue
put into the mouth of Ἄγνοια,[3] personified as a goddess, in
which the author explains what must have been the events
in Act I. Probably it was an introductory speech to Act II.
It is remarkable in many ways. Menander's contemporary,
Diphilus, wrote a comedy with the same title, but Menander
had deeper reasons for his choice of such a goddess to deliver
this particular speech. He at once introduces his audience to
the very spirit of Comedy itself. If Tragedy is the story of
the ruin of a character in conflict with the will of Heaven as
revealed by oracles and soothsayers, Comedy is the story of
man's struggle with the greatest foe of civilized society, Misapprehension or Ignorance, and its concomitant, Chance;
Comedy is precisely the revelation of character when it is
brought into contact with the unknown possibilities in the
complex circumstances which are the essence of city life.
Again, the goddess in this play states that the previous events

---

[1] l. 279 ὅρκος, πόθος.   [2] l. 120 ἄσμενος.

[3] 'Misapprehension' is Mr. Capps's rendering (*Four Plays of
Menander*. p. 134). See his development of the idea. He compares
Menander's creation of Ἔλεγχος in another prologue, the spirit which
brings the truth to light. Lucian, *Pseudol.* 4, is the authority.

had taken place in order that a special motive might be created for the act which was to set the whole play in motion. It was ignorance which drove the soldier to maltreat his mistress: ignorance which betrayed him to an unjust act: ignorance was the 'notable vice in him upon which her cunning was to work'.[1] Again, this insult was the one means whereby good could be made to come out of evil,[2] and that only by the interposition of a god. The evident sincerity of the lines makes it unlikely that the poet is merely ridiculing the prologues of Euripides.

The scene of the play is almost certainly Corinth. Two children, Moschio and Glycera, had been found by some woman not named. She kept the girl, but gave the boy to her neighbour, Myrrhina, a rich woman, who had no son. As the girl grew up, war and domestic troubles compelled the foster-mother to give her to Polemo, a hot-tempered Corinthian youth,[3] but she took the precaution of telling her about her brother, in case the girl should be left friendless if she herself died. Polemo had bought a house next to Myrrhina's in the city, from which Glycera could easily note the wild life her brother was leading. When her foster-mother died, Glycera was one evening standing at the doors of the house, when Moschio ran up to her and embraced her. She returned his caresses with equal affection, but was seen by Polemo, who, in a fit of jealousy, revenged himself by shearing off his mistress's hair. She ran away to Myrrhina's house, and at this point the action begins.

Next morning Polemo sends his servant Sosia from the country residence to the town, ostensibly to fetch his cloak, really to bring him news of Glycera, of whose maltreatment he repents himself. Sosia watches Doris, Glycera's maid, knock at Myrrhina's door. A lacuna makes the action uncertain; Myrrhina, however, shelters Glycera, while Davus, Moschio's servant, goes off to find his master and acquaint

---

[1] ll. 42-4   πάντα δ' ἐξεκάετο
       ταῦθ' ἕνεκα τοῦ μέλλοντος, εἰς ὀργὴν ἵνα
       οὗτος ἀφίκητ'.

[2] l. 49 διὰ γὰρ θεοῦ καὶ τὸ κακὸν εἰς ἀγαθὸν ῥέπει.   Comp. ll. 442-3.

[3] l. 8 σφοδρός. l. 44 οὐ φύσει τοιοῦτον ὄντα is corrupt.

him with the good news that his fancied mistress is in his mother's house.

The next scene opens with a diverting dialogue between Moschio and Davus. The former at first refuses to believe the news, convinced that this is only one more of Davus's tricks. Eventually he professes to credit his word, sending him in to find out whether his mother would like to see him, and pluming himself on his powers of impressing the female heart. He is rudely awakened by Davus's return, who assures him that his welcome was most unkind. Instead of her being glad that her son knew of Glycera's presence, she upbraided Davus for telling him. Moschio at once accuses Davus of playing him false, but Davus, after an effort, induces him to believe that his mother suggested to him an absence of two or three days[1] until matters had calmed down. Both then pass into the house to make their preparations for departure.

Sosia now reappears, again sent for the cloak. Passing into the house he finds Glycera gone, and rushes out just in time to see Doris coming from Myrrhina's. In a fury he tries to force an entrance into it, but is resisted by Myrrhina's door-keeper. Threatening a siege of these town mice he turns round on Doris and accuses her of being privy to the whole plot. The action is slightly interrupted by another lacuna, after which Pataecus (who proves afterwards to be the father of Moschio and Glycera) is found in conversation with Polemo and Sosia, who are threatening to force an entrance. Sosia is induced to abandon the mad project, whereupon Pataecus speaks reasonably to Polemo, who is so enraged that he cannot control his utterance.[2] He points out that Glycera is her own mistress; she can therefore be induced to return only by persuasion; if any man has outraged him, his only course is

---

[1] ll. 153-4:

$$\epsilon\grave{\iota} \ \sigma\grave{\upsilon} \ \tau\rho\epsilon\hat{\iota}s \ \mathring{\eta} \ \tau\acute{\epsilon}\tau\tau\alpha\rho\alpha s$$
$$\mathring{\eta}\mu\acute{\epsilon}\rho\alpha s \ \beta o\acute{\upsilon}\lambda\epsilon\iota \ \pi\rho o\sigma\acute{\epsilon}\xi\epsilon\iota \ \tau\iota s.$$

The middle letters of βούλει are not quite certain. Moschio in reply says he would be taking a very long walk—περιπατεῖν ποιεῖς με περίπατον πολύν τινα, while Davus assures him he has the ἐφόδια for that time. May we not then read βαδιεῖ = 'if you will only take a walk'? βαδιεῖ occurs in *Hero*, p. 8.   [2] l. 239 μὴ βόα.

to get satisfaction through the law-courts. Polemo, in reply, begs Pataecus to act as ambassador, as he has often met her and spoken with her before,[1] but first insists on his seeing some of the splendid clothes she was in the habit of wearing.[2]

Moschio now reappears. Scattering the wretched gang of Sosia's fellow-slaves, he relates how he again sent Davus with a message to his mother, but that the servant took the opportunity to devour a breakfast prepared for Myrrhina while Moschio was delighting his imagination with the thoughts of the terms upon which he would meet the girl.

Unfortunately, when the action of the play most needs elucidation, another lacuna occurs. Glycera is shown on the stage in conversation with Pataecus, to whom she justifies her conduct towards Moschio. In all probability she was aware that Pataecus, her acquaintance, had consented to act as mediator, and decided to meet him outside through consideration for Myrrhina, to whom the interview could not but bring pain.[3] To Pataecus's suggestion that she should return at once to Polemo she returns a firm refusal, pointing out that his treatment of her had been unfit for a servant.[4] She demands the restoration of certain jewels belonging to her parents. Pataecus ridicules the suggestion, but a firm reply from the girl suffices. Doris is sent for and requested to bring the chest containing these jewels. When they are produced, Pataecus at once recognizes them as belonging to his dead wife. The style of this portion of the play rises in dignity to the level of tragedy, to correspond with the importance of the subject. Pataecus asks about the second child, but Glycera refuses to tell the truth, as she had promised secrecy to Myrrhina,[5] probably to save her from complications with her husband. The scene of the place where the children were exposed is described.[6] Pataecus then acknowledges Glycera to be his daughter, defending his abandonment of his children on the ground of the death of his wife and the loss of a ship which contained his merchandise. Moschio meanwhile had

---

[1] ll. 258–9.   [2] ll. 269–72.
[3] Sudhaus believes that Myrrhina's husband ejected Glycera!
[4] l. 319.   [5] ll. 360–1.   [6] l. 367.

been a silent spectator of the scene. At the outset he was quickly convinced that Glycera was his sister,[1] but believed that Myrrhina was his and her mother. On hearing further details of the ornaments found with the children he rushes out, and completes the 'Recognition' by finding that Pataecus is his father.

In the final scene Polemo reappears, lamenting the loss of Glycera. He at last knows that Moschio was her brother. Doris however comforts him with the assurance that she will return, and receives the promise of her freedom in consequence. Glycera had secretly cherished an affection for him, and the two are united by Pataecus, who gives a handsome dowry with her, finding a bride for his son. The fragments end fittingly after Glycera's remark that Polemo's mad act had led to happiness.

In the play the most striking personage is Glycera, whom Menander rightly chose for the heroine. Her character is almost Shakespearian—certainly it is unique among the creations of Menander that have come down to us. Her appearance is hinted at by Polemo; she was a striking figure, to whom her attire lent majesty.[2] Her actions bear out the impression of strength which his description conveys. She is brave enough to risk public criticism to find a brother; she is strong enough to break with one she loves on the ground of ill treatment. In justifying her conduct to Pataecus she shows foresight and sagacity far beyond her years; this scene so fortunately preserved is a masterpiece.[3] It would not be easy to produce a parallel to the searching analysis of motive in a female character of the New Comedy. When Pataecus ventures to ridicule her for demanding her jewellery she administers the quiet rebuke, 'I know my own business best'.[4] In every way she is worthy of a place only a little below that held by another girl, young, calm, patient, and strong, working under a curiously similar motive—Helena, the heroine of *All's Well*.

[1] ll. 345-7.
[2] ll. 269-71, esp. the last line,
$$\tau\grave{o}\ \mu\acute{\epsilon}\gamma\epsilon\theta os\ \delta\acute{\eta}\pi o\upsilon\theta\epsilon\nu\ \tilde{\eta}\nu$$
$$\mathring{a}\xi\iota o\nu\ \mathring{\iota}\delta\epsilon\tilde{\iota}\nu.$$
[3] ll. 312-18.
[4] l. 326 $\mathring{\epsilon}\gamma\tilde{\wphi}\delta a\ \tau\mathring{a}\mu'\ \mathring{a}\rho\iota\sigma\theta'$.

The other characters do not stand out quite so vividly. Pataecus is the counterfoil to the mad passion of Polemo. He advocates reason and legal redress, not violence, for a supposed injury. We find it difficult to pardon his wilful exposure of his children through fear of poverty, but no doubt his action would satisfy the morality of his age. Polemo is well handled. The violence of his nature is completely under the control of the calm reason of Glycera, except for the mad fit of jealousy which Menander ascribed directly to the goddess.[1] It is the highest compliment to him that he won the affection of the wonderful girl who consented to live with him; we have no doubt that a few years of matrimony will make him a respectable citizen. Moschio and Davus conform to the type of fast young man and cunning servant; the former is vain where the sex is concerned,[2] imagining himself to be irresistible;[3] it is a master-stroke which turned the supposed sweetheart into a sister; he certainly got more than he deserved even then.

Sosia and Doris would seem to demand a separate discussion. The former is to all appearances a mere 'roaring boy', understudy to his master, or rather more violent still;[4] his language is as inexhaustible as are his spirits, and he is a good leader of the wretched gang whom Moschio scatters at a breath. Yet a deeper examination reveals in him the same features of goodness which must have been in Polemo; it is a nature above a slave's which refused to go back to his master with tidings worse than the truth, because of the sheer pity he felt for him.[5] Doris is just as faithful to her mistress, and just as courageous;[6] she no more fears Sosia than Glycera does Polemo, and she pities her for associating with a soldier who is, as his kind, lawless and faithless.[7] She thoroughly deserves her freedom, and is worthy of the confidence of her

[1] l. 44. [2] l. 112 οὐκ ἀηδής . . . εἴμ' ἰδεῖν.
[3] l. 113 προσφιλής. Comp. also ll. 297-300.
[4] l. 221, to Polemo, ἧττον μεθύεις γάρ.
[5] l. 168 εἰ μή γε παντάπασιν αὐτὸν ἠλέουν. [6] ll. 207-11.
[7] ll. 65-7   δυστυχὴς
ἥτις στρατιώτην ἔλαβεν ἄνδρα· παράνομοι
ἅπαντες, οὐδὲν πιστόν.

mistress and of the applause of her audience in a play in which the women easily bear the palm.

The last of the fragments found at Aphroditopolis form a portion of a play of uncertain title. Two young men, Chaereas and Moschio, love the same girl. Moschio tried to induce Chaereas to give her up and marry his own sister, but Chaereas could not well do so without insulting the girl's father, Cleaenetus. This last person appears to inform them that Moschio has become the father of a child by his daughter, and that he himself intended his daughter for Moschio. Chaereas's difficulty being now settled, he is no doubt free to marry Moschio's sister.

When Laches, the father of Moschio, hears the news of his son's marriage he imagines himself to be the victim of some cunning plot concocted by the two young men, and seems to display a levity unsuited to his years. The plot certainly offers scope for ingenious treatment.

The next play, the Γεωργός, was known from half a dozen quotations; the Geneva fragment, discovered in 1897 in Egypt, contributes nearly ninety consecutive lines which are rather puzzling. It seems to be difficult to fix the characters of the play as the fragments describe them. Myrrhina had borne two children to Cleaenetus, who lived on his estate in the country. The son worked for his father, though he did not know his relationship to him. One day Cleaenetus, a harsh man,[1] while digging in the vineyard, cut his leg. Myrrhina's son tended him well; in return Cleaenetus inquired about his family, and, finding he had a sister living in deep poverty, felt a human touch[2] and offered to marry her. This news is brought by Davus, who was sent on before with some farm produce for the marriage ceremony, his master intending to follow almost immediately. When Myrrhina hears the news, she is obliged to reveal to Philinna, an old gossip of hers, the reasons why Cleaenetus cannot marry the girl. Apart from the fact that Cleaenetus was her father, her daughter had been seduced by a young man who might reasonably be

---

[1] l. 66 σκληρός.   [2] l. 71 ἔπαθέν τι κοινόν.

expected to dread her brother's resentment. The fragment ends here. Cleaenetus and Myrrhina will obviously be reunited, and the daughter will be married to her lover.

But the real difficulty is in the opening lines. A young man appears on the stage stating that he has just returned from Corinth, and finds that his father has arranged a marriage for him with his step-sister by a second wife. The youth cannot escape the marriage, yet cannot abandon his sweetheart, whose name has disappeared. He stands in hesitation before a door, as he does not know whether the girl's brother has returned from the country.[1] Another youth in the country had been previously mentioned.[2] In the quotations from Stobaeus and Orion a character Gorgias appears. How should these persons be distributed? It seems as if this young man for whom the marriage is arranged was the lover of Myrrhina's daughter, and that the youth 'in the country' mentioned twice is the same person, Myrrhina's son; if not, the play promises to be rather complicated. Gorgias may be either the youth's father, who is arranging the marriage, or Myrrhina's son.

The little touches that endear Menander to us are in evidence in this fragment. Myrrhina, the wronged mother, is willing to forgive an injury;[3] Cleaenetus has a human heart under a rough exterior.

The Berlin fragment[4] contains about a hundred lines of a play which has been identified as part of the Κιθαριστής. A young man has just married a free girl whom he has temporarily left behind, probably for business reasons, to follow him. She has for some reason not yet appeared, and her husband suspects some accident at sea. Meanwhile he goes to the market-place with a friend, to whom he promises to tell the whole story.

In the next scene a father appears to meet his son Moschio — a most unusual event, as the son generally avoided him. The father rather likes him for proving by his evasiveness that he is his genuine son, and that his wife is therefore in this respect

---

[1] l. 18.   [2] l. 4.   [3] l. 28 χαιρέτω.
[4] *Berlin. Klass. Texte*, v. 2, 115.

no offender.[1] Moschio now explains the reason for this meeting ; he has come to man's estate ; his father wishes him to marry.[2] Moschio however has just returned from Ephesus, where he met at a festival[3] of Artemis the daughter of Phanias, who had gone there to recover some debts. His father is not at all anxious for the match.

How the play was worked out it is impossible to say. It contains marks of Menander's tone of thought ;[4] the father reminds us of the astonishingly young Capulet in *Romeo and Juliet*.

The *Oxyrhynchus Papyri* also contain fragments of the Κόλαξ,[5] a play which Terence says that he utilized in his *Eunuchus* (Prol. 30-2) :

> Colax Menandri est; in ea est parasitus Colax
> et miles gloriosus : eas se non negat
> personas transtulisse in Eunuchum suam.

A young man, Phidias, had been left by his father in Athens on a short allowance. His mistress is in the possession of a *leno*, and he consults with her maid Doris how he can redeem her. His rival is a soldier, Bias, who has suddenly become rich. Phidias appears to be conversing with his old παιδαγωγός, who assures him that such wealth must have been acquired unjustly (' I should like to expose him ', bursts out Phidias), by flattery, which has proved the ruin of the great ones of the earth.[6] In the next scene the *leno* is talking with some one over his difficulties: he is unwilling to let Phidias have the girl, because she is profitable to him, and he is afraid that Bias, the *Miles Gloriosus*, will come with a

---

[1] ll. 59-62, a most amusing passage :
καὶ γὰρ αὐτὸς ἐγενόμην
εἰς τῶν δυναμένων οἰκίαν μικρὰν ποεῖν.
οὐκ ἠδίκηκεν ἡ γυνὴ κατὰ τοῦτό γε,
ἀλλ' ἐξ ἐμοῦ 'στιν· οὐθὲν ἀγαθὸν γοῦν ποεῖ.
[2] l. 79.　　　　　　　　　　[3] l. 95 δειπνοφορία.
[4] ἀτύχημα, l. 47 ; φρονήσεως, l. 80.
[5] *Oxyrh. Pap.* iii. 409; x. 1237.
[6] ll. 59-63　ὅσοι τύραννοι πώποθ', ὅστις ἡγεμὼν
μέγας, σατράπης, φρούραρχος, οἰκιστὴς τόπου,
στρατηγός, οὐ γὰρ ἀλλὰ τοὺς τελέως λέγω
ἀπολωλότας νῦν, τοῦτ' ἀνῄρηκεν μόνον,
οἱ κόλακες· οὗτοι δ' εἰσὶν αὐτοῖς ἄθλιοι.

band of bullies and carry her off; and that the young lover
will come with another band—

> πρόσεισιν ἐξήκονθ' ἑταίρους παραλαβών,
> ὅσους 'Οδυσσεὺς ἦλθεν εἰς Τροίαν ἔχων,
> βοῶν, ἀπειλῶν

(with which may be compared the scene in *Eunuchus* iv. 7,
where Thraso with his men prepares to attack the house of
Thais); and lastly he fears the expenses of a lawsuit.

It is plain that in the end the soldier is defeated, and
Phidias wins the girl.

The subject of the play, the violence of the actors, the strain
of free-thought [1] and bitterness,[2] and the nascent sententiousness all point to the conclusion that this is one of Menander's
early pieces.

The Κωνειαζόμεναι [3] (poison-drinkers) survives in some
twenty lines only. A youth, evidently in despair, learns the
happy news that his suit is likely to prosper: his sweetheart's
father has relented, offering him a handsome dowry with his
daughter. Then a second character comes on the stage, and
makes a speech which is yet another integral part of Menander's philosophy. Fortune is not always unkind: it is
useless to revile her; we need never despair.[4]

The Μισούμενος [5] is a mutilated fragment of forty-four lines.
The leading character was already known from other sources
to be Thrasonides, who by his rude and overbearing character
had alienated his mistress, Crateia, daughter of Demeas. The
latest fragments probably represent him imploring his father
to secure for him a reconciliation with Demeas and his

---

[1] ll. 26-7:

> (συλλαμβάνειν γε τοῖς) πονηροῖς τοὺς θεούς·
> (ἀγαθοὶ γὰρ ὄντες οὐδὲ)ν ἀγαθὸν πράττομεν.

[2] l. 42, the famous οὐδεὶς ἐπλούτησεν ταχέως δίκαιος ὤν.

[3] Papyrus at Dorpat.

[4] ll. 13–21, esp. 18-19 μηθεὶς πρὸς θεῶν . . . λίαν ἀθυμήσῃ ποτέ.

[5] *Oxyrh. Pap.* vii, No. 1013. It is very likely that some thirty
mutilated lines in the *Berlin. Klass. Texte*, v. 2, 113, belong to the
Μισούμενος: A. Körte in *Archiv f. Papyrusforschung*, vi. 231. *Oxyrh.
Pap.* xiii, No. 1605, contains more scraps, and probably *Sitzungsb. d. Berl.
Akad.*, 1918, 747-9 (see Grenfell and Hunt on *Oxyrh. Pap.* 1605).

daughter. Thus the situation is much like that of Polemo and Glycera in the Περικειρομένη.

The Περινθία[1] is more interesting. Terence informs us that this play and the *Andria* were written on the same subject, but in quite dissimilar styles.[2] The Oxyrhynchus fragment shows us Davus, a slave, who had called his master slothful and empty-headed, and was now being burnt out of his place of refuge, an altar, to which he had fled for sanctuary. We are reminded of the scene in Plautus's *Rudens*, iii. 4, where Labrax threatens to burn alive the two girls who have taken refuge in this way (l. 761 *Volcanum adducam*, to l. 770). The violence of such a scene is a valuable indication of the earliest methods which Menander employed; it would certainly not have been so presented in the later plays. Grenfell and Hunt point out that the scene in the *Thesmophoria-zusae* 726 sqq., in which the women make preparations to burn Mnesilochus, is not unlike this.

A fragment of an unusual nature, dealing with Menander, is printed as *Oxyrhynchus Papyri*, x. 1235. It formed part of a roll which contained apparently a list of Menander's plays in alphabetical order, with an historical note on their date and production; then an abstract of each story, and lastly a literary appreciation. The only parts preserved are part of the plot of the Ἱέρεια, and the historical note on the Ἴμβριοι and the beginning of the plot. Grenfell and Hunt accept Wilamowitz's supplement to the account of the Ἱέρεια: τὸ δὲ δρᾶμα τῶν ἀρίστων. The story was as follows: a man had married a priestess, the issue of the marriage being a son. The parents being estranged for some reason not specified, the boy was bought up by some neighbours together with a genuine son of their own, a younger boy. A slave pretended to be possessed, in order to discover the truth. Having done so, he told the priestess's husband, but made a mistake in the

---

[1] *Oxyrh. Pap.* vi. 855.
[2] Ter. *And.* Prol. 9 sqq.:
   Menander fecit Andriam et Perinthiam:
   qui utramvis recte norit, ambas noverit;
   non ita sunt dissimili argumento, sed tamen
   dissimili oratione sunt factae ac stilo.

children, naming the wrong boy as his son. This latter warned
his supposed brother, who avoided his real father on the ground
of madness. The younger son had fallen in love with the
priestess's daughter, the elder with his foster-sister. Eventually
the two families are united in marriage : each youth marries
his sweetheart, and the priestess returns to her husband.

The temper of Menander is one that would dislike the
enthusiast and the fanatic ; and we are not surprised to find,
in a fragment of the play which we already possessed, lines
which speak of the priests of Cybele in a tone of grave
contempt :

εἰ γὰρ ἕλκει τὸν θεὸν
τοῖς κυμβάλοις ἄνθρωπος εἰς ὃ βούλεται,
ὁ τοῦτο ποιῶν ἐστι μείζων τοῦ θεοῦ,

just as he said with equal severity in the Ἡνίοχος :

οὐδείς μ᾽ ἀρέσκει περιπατῶν ἔξω θεὸς
μετὰ γραός.

All that we learn about the plot of the Ἴμβριοι is, that two
poor men, living in partnership at Imbros and working indus-
triously on land and sea, married twin sisters.

We possess large portions of fifty-five lines from the opening of the Φάσμα ('The Ghost'), preserved in a MS. of the
fourth century at Petrograd. An outline of the play was
already known from Donatus's note on the Eunuchus of
Terence, l. 9.

A girl, the daughter of a woman who had married the
father of Phidias, the hero of the play, was kept secluded in
the next-door neighbour's house by her mother, who had
made a passage between the houses, decorated it with greenery,
and given out that it was a chapel. Thus the girl was able
to visit her mother, and was one day discovered by Phidias,
who was at first alarmed, thinking that he had seen a ghost.
But he learnt the truth and fell in love with the girl, and the
play ended with a wedding. Part of the Prologue is preserved, and then a scene follows between Phidias and probably
a παιδαγωγός. Phidias is in a state of brooding melancholy
and is reasoned with by the παιδαγωγός, who rallies him on

his idle and luxurious life in words of wit and wisdom. Even
the mutilation of the lines has not defaced the clear outline of
this vivid scene.

Such are the treasures which have come chiefly from the
tombs and earthen vessels of Egypt.

In order to estimate the value of the fragments which have
come down to us, it would seem worth our while to consider
the principles upon which Menander worked. He is effective
because of the solidity and strength of the foundations which
underlie his art. To him the essence of life as he looked at it
was the important influence which Chance could exercise. In
every play the workings of Chance are everywhere plainly
made the mainspring of the action. Thus, in the *Hero* it was
famine which compelled Tibeius to mortgage his ' children ' to
Laches.[1] In the 'Επιτρέποντες chance made Smicrines the
judge[2] about the child whom Davus found. Demeas, in the
Σαμία, went into his store-room by a mere accident.[3] Cleaenetus, in the Γεωργός, quite as accidentally cut his leg, on
which accident the play depends. In the Κιθαριστής the
same influence is at work[4]; in the Κόλαξ the soldier Bias is
compared to the proverbial luckless ass.[5] This ' chance ' is
merely the measure of our ignorance; hence Ignorance, the
hidden influence that directs the events of the Περικειρομένη,
is the goddess which is really the very controlling deity of
Menander's system, the tutelary of his works.

This philosophy is summed up for us in the passage in the
'Επιτρέποντες to which attention has already been directed.
It is concealed under a veil of humour, no doubt, but it is
Menander's guiding principle all the same. The gods cannot
look after a thousand cities, each with ten thousand inhabitants ;
they would be tired out. Yet it is not true to say that they
do not care for us at all. Rather, they care for us so much
that they have given a sentinel to guard the fort of our reason,
namely, our personality. This god within us punishes all who
maltreat him by freakish or ignorant deeds, holding each

[1] l. 3.   [2] l. 6 ἀγαθῇ τύχῃ.
[3] l. 14 ἔτυχον εἰσελθών.
[4] l. 47 ἀτύχημα.   [5] l. 31.

responsible for success or failure.[1] As a corollary, Menander
insists that it is useless to shake one's fist at Fortune, and to
lose heart ; [2] the best thing to do is to use ordinary prudence.[3]
Accordingly the personages whom Menander intended to
exemplify his ideal of dramatic excellence are Syriscus and
Habrotonon [4] in the Ἐπιτρέποντες, Glycera in the Περικειρομένη,[5] and Moschio in the Κιθαριστής.[6] The material upon
which they exercise their intelligence is what would with bad
handling be an ἀτύχημα [7], making them ἀτυχεῖς,[8] or more
commonly δυστυχεῖς.[9] Such mishandling may spring from
a violent fit of temper, which nearly ruined Polemo's hope of
happiness, or pride, which brought Charisius to the verge of
domestic misery [10]—acts of men who are headstrong (προπετεῖς).

The moral code of these plays is in frequent collision with
the best ethical teaching of modern times. Incontinence he
generally pardons ; apart from the numerous cases of young
men leading young girls astray, he makes Demeas in the
Σαμία harbour a mistress. The former class of acts he might
possibly excuse on the ground of inexperience [11] or heredity ; [12]
the latter has no defence at all in a man who otherwise com-
mands our respect. Here we touch upon Menander's standard of condemnation, always the surest sign of the morality
of an age. He has an easy toleration for all acts but those

[1] ll. 545 ft., esp. 552 :

"οὐκ ἄρα φροντίζουσιν ἡμῶν οἱ θεοί"
φήσεις—ἑκάστῳ τὸν τρόπον συνῴκισαν
φρούραρχον· οὗτος ἐνδελεχὴς παρὼν φύλαξ
ἐπέτριψεν, ἂν αὐτῷ κακῶς χρῆσθαι δοκῇ,
ἕτερον δ' ἔσωσεν· οὗτός ἐσθ' ἡμῖν θεὸς
ὅ τ' αἴτιος καὶ τοῦ καλῶς καὶ τοῦ κακῶς
πράττειν ἑκάστῳ· τοῦτον ἱλάσκου ποῶν
μηδὲν ἄτοπον μηδ' ἀμαθές, ἵνα πράττῃς καλῶς.

It is strange how this lovely passage found none to admire it in antiquity.
It is practically the essence of Bishop Butler's system and is at the bottom
of all prudential philosophy.

[2] Κωνει. 12, 19.
[3] Comp. Ἐπιτρ. 126-8 :

ὄντ' ἐπισφαλῆ φύσει
τὸν βίον ἁπάντων τῇ προνοίᾳ δεῖ, πάτερ,
τηρεῖν, πρὸ πολλῶν ταῦθ' ὁρῶντ' ἐξ ὧν ἔνι.

[4] ll. 341-3.   [5] l. 309 ἀφρόνως ἔχειν.
[6] l. 80 φρονήσεως γὰρ δεῖ.   [7] Ἐπιτρ. 493, 500 ; Σαμ. 136.
[8] Ἐπιτρ. 497.   [9] Seven times.   [10] Ἐπιτρ. 492 μέγαλα φυσᾷς.
[11] Σαμ. 126.   [12] Κιθ. 59-62.

which have only a social meaning; domestic irregularities
he seems to regard as not social; they therefore imply to
him no 'injustice'. It is instructive to review rapidly the
acts which he arraigns as unjust: they will be found to be
limited almost entirely to offences against the freeborn.
Thus, in the ' Ἐπιτρέποντες Davus is robbing a child evidently
freeborn of the one proof which was available of his status;[1]
Syriscus gets a verdict because he proceeds against this act.[2]
Glycera, really a free woman, had suffered this injustice[3] from
a man who would recover control over her by another 'unjust'
attack on another free woman's house.[4]   On the other hand,
Demeas willingly admits that Moschio, even in corrupting his
mistress, committed no offence against him,[5] whereas a refusal
in the same youth to marry a citizen's daughter would be such
an act.[6]

Menander's subject-matter was exclusively the love-plot.
He treats the theme with a fertility of resource to which the
best parallel is the Spanish comedy of *Capa y Espada*.[7]   In
both the same subject is dealt with in an infinite variety of
detail.   Very often the plot was consummated by a 'Recognition'.   It is strange that this dramatic trick never wearied the
Athenian audience.   It had no less an authority behind it
than the *Odyssey*; had been freely used by the tragedians;
and became a part of the stock-in-trade of the Romantic
writers long after Comedy ceased to be written;[8] in fact it
seems to have been almost as integral a part of the Greek
comic tradition as the legends were of tragedy.

The stage resources which Menander employs were more
numerous than those of earlier dramatists.   The argument of
the ῟Ηρως mentions nine characters; the Ἐπιτρέποντες contains
ten, the Περικειρομένη eleven.   There were at least two houses
in most plays; sometimes three were visible to the audience.

[1] Called picturesquely τῆς σωτηρίας ἐλπίδα, l. 122.
[2] l. 140 ἐπεξιόντος τἀδικεῖν.   [3] Περικ. 68.   [4] l. 252.
[5] Σαμ. 113.   [6] l. 238.
[7] The comedy of 'The Cloak and Sword'.   The subjects, the society,
and the ingenious intricacy of the plots are similar.   See Butler Clarke,
Spanish Literature, p. 163.
[8] e. g. Heliodorus, Achilles Tatius.

The movements of the actors were practically unimpeded; forcible ejections, violent entrances into houses, and even sieges, were not impossible. The choruses marked the divisions of the plays. One passage in particular is of some value as proving that the unities were no more observed in Comedy than they were in Tragedy, and that the extreme classical tradition in these matters is too rigorous: in the Ἐπιτρέποντες Syriscus is obliged to wait at least a whole day to get the mystery of the child cleared up.[1]

The growth of Menander's art is quite clearly marked in these fragments.[2] The work of a young man is evident in the energy and even violence of the Περινθία, and perhaps in the Σαμία. The gradual growth of a sound philosophy is well shown by a contrast between the somewhat cynical tone of the Κόλαξ and the altogether sane view of life taken in the Κωνειαζόμεναι, finding its consummation in the Ἐπιτρέποντες. The sententiousness of Menander, as we knew him before the recent discoveries, might find an easy parallel if Shakespeare had survived only in books of quotations or in anthologies; the fragments however show surprisingly little of it. The most striking instance is in the Κόλαξ,[3] perhaps still another argument for the early date of the play.

Everywhere we are made conscious of a great literary tradition behind this wonderful language. Proverbs disappear where reasoned knowledge is valued. The very felicity of his speech was certain to make Menander a mine of quotations,

---

[1] l. 197 O. αὔριον δέ. Σ. καταμενῶ.

[2] In an admirable criticism of the new Menander Papyri, Sir Frederick Kenyon observes with justice: 'The plays give the impression that they have the prime merit of being effective on the stage. The dialogue is brisk and lively, though it has not the verbal jokes and jibes of Aristophanes. The action moves rapidly; the scenes are of no great length; the characters on the stage are continually in motion; and the audience is given little time to cool down and consider the situation in cold blood' (*Quarterly Review*, vol. ccviii, p. 341). Mr. H. P. Richards, in the *Classical Quarterly*, vol. ii, p. 132, finding a want of comic force and of marked excellence of style, is more measured in his praise. He recalls the story in Plutarch, *Moral.* 347 F: a friend remarked to Menander that the Dionysia were near, and Menander's play was not ready. He replied: 'It is ready: I have finished the plot; I have only to write the lines' (τὰ στιχίδια). A similar story was told of the elder Dumas.

But the criticisms of these two scholars supplement and do not exclude each other.   [3] ll. 42–5.

but the value of his style is increased by the delicate yet unmistakable reminiscences which it contains. There is a distinct Aeschylean ring in Habrotonon's language when she decides on the act which was to make her fortune ;[1] and the scene in the Περινθία, in which Davus is being burnt out of his refuge at the altar, is almost a parody of the fettering of Prometheus at the opening of the *Prometheus Vinctus*: compare Περ. 10 sqq. :

περίθετ᾽ ἐν κύκλῳ ταχύ.
νυνί γ᾽ ἐπ]ίδειξαι, Δᾶε, τὴν πανουργίαν,
τέχνην τιν᾽ εὑρὼν διαφυγών τ᾽ ἐνθένδε με.

with *Prom. Vinct.* 52 :

οὔκουν ἐπείξει δεσμὰ τῷδε περιβαλεῖν ;

and 85, 86 :

αὐτὸν γάρ σε δεῖ προμηθέως,
ὅτῳ τρόπῳ τῆσδ᾽ ἐκκυλισθήσει τύχης.

There is, as we would have expected, a direct acknowledgement of the immense debt which the author owed to Euripides. Apart from the explicit quotation from the Αὔγη,[2] there is a reference to the whole body of 'Recognition' drama (especially perhaps to Sophocles' *Tyro*), and that in the mouth of a slave,[3] and to the romantic drama from the lips of Demeas.[4] The trial scene at the opening of the 'Επιτρέποντες is simply Euripidean throughout, and based upon the *Alope*, as may be seen from the summary in Hyginus, *Fab.* 187 ; while the very language of the tragedians is copied in the Περικειρομένη when the comedy is closely imitating the tragic device of 'Recognition'.[5] The cross-questioning in this passage quite calls to mind the *Oedipus Tyrannus* 1025 sqq. One other passage unmistakably recalls Demosthenes in words that breathe the great patriot's sorrow for his country's miseries.[6]

---

[1] 'Επιτρ. ll. 338-9 :
φίλη Πειθοῖ, παροῦσα σύμμαχος
πόει κατορθοῦν τοὺς λόγους οὓς ἂν λέγω.
Comp. *Agam.* l. 973 Ζεῦ Ζεῦ τέλειε, τὰς ἐμὰς εὐχὰς τέλει.
[2] 'Επιτρ. 583-4 = Eur. *Fr.* 920 N.
[3] Ib. 108 f.
[4] Σαμ. 245.
[5] Περικ. 338-97.
[6] Ib. 280-2 :
πολλῶν γεγονότων ἀθλίων κατὰ τὸν χρόνον
τὸν νῦν—φορὰ γὰρ γέγονε τούτων καλὴ
ἐν ἅπασι τοῖς Ἕλλησι δι᾽ ὅτι δήποτε.

One more point is perhaps worth mention. It is remarkable that nearly every play contains at least one character or one scene drawn from the country districts. The "Ηρως is the story of a woodcutter's love for a shepherd's daughter. The 'Επιτρέποντες are a shepherd and a charcoal-burner. The twins in the Περικειρομένη were exposed in a country district, an accurate description of which is an accessory proof of their parentage. The Γεωργός names itself. A remarkable taunt is hurled at a gate-keeper by a country-bred slave.[1] The call of the country was strong for those whose city life had passed under the control of the Macedonian.

But the greatest treasure of all is the revelation of Menander's own character. There are wonderful touches of tenderness [2] which interpret to us the man himself. On these fragments is stamped indelibly the personality of one who does noble nature credit. Like Euripides, he found his grain where contemporaries saw nothing but husks. He discovered a slave with a free man's generous instincts, and named him Davus in the "Ηρως. He saw that pity could live even under the rough exterior of a bully, and redeemed Sosia in the Περικειρομένη. His eye discerned a noble girl, patient under insult, faithful to him who was her bone and flesh, and he created Pamphila. The same loyalty he discovered in the Samian Chrysis. Looking yet again into the perfect pattern of womanhood, he drew Glycera, sweetest of them all. None but a nature to whom these things were of value would find time to describe them; if they are of worth to us as well, Menander shall by no means lose his reward.

A few fragments of other comedies have been discovered. Their scanty nature makes it unprofitable to discuss them at any length. They are variations of the usual theme. The first [3] seems to describe the flight of a young man with his servant, aided by Demeas, a man of generous instincts.[4] The comic note is firmly struck at the outset.[5] The flight is

---

[1] Περικ. 204–5 πόλιν οἰκοῦντας.
[2] Γεωρ. 71 ἔπαθέν τι κοινόν.
[3] *Hibeh Pap.*, i. 6.
[4] l. 36.
[5] ll. 37–8 :

ἀλλὰ τῇ Τύχῃ
οὐδὲν διαφέρειν φαίνεθ' ὃν ποιεῖ κακῶς.

perhaps due to the father's opposition to his marriage with Demeas's daughter. Demeas recognizes that the two families must henceforth be enemies; subsequently he seems to discover that his daughter has borne a child. There are distinct reminiscences of the Σαμία of Menander. The author is not identified.

In another fragment[1] a slave, Strobilus, seems to have had a stroke of fortune in Egypt,[2] which he describes in lines of some literary merit.[3] Blass and Grenfell and Hunt think it likely that the comedy may be by Philemon, and that it may have been the original of Plautus's *Aulularia*.

Once again we have the discovery of a brother and a sister by the familiar evidence of clothes[4] in an Egyptian imitation of the Περικειρομένη. Fresh ground is broken in another series of fragments.[5] Phaedimus, seeing his sweetheart escape from her mother into the house of his friend Niceratus, accuses him of treachery; their speeches are preserved in a passage full of feeling.[6] Chaerestratus, Phaedimus's slave, is about to set matters right when the fragments end. Koerte thinks that the style and metre are not Menander's, and may be based upon its originals.

Another fragment[7] is rather like Terence's *Andria*.

One prologue,[8] a metrical argument followed by a prologue differing from it,[9] complete the material which it is possible to read in entire lines.

A commentary on Demosthenes by Didymus has preserved

[1] *Hibeh Pap.* i. 5.   [2] l. 7 νομαρχ . . .
[3] ll. 51-4:

νῦν οἶδ' ἀκριβῶς διότι τῆς οἰκουμένης
ἱερὰ σαφῶς αὕτη 'στιν ἡ χώρα μόνη,
κἀνθάδε κατῳκήκασι πάντες οἱ θεοί,
καὶ νῦν ἔτ' εἰσὶ καὶ γεγόνασιν ἐνθάδε.

[4] *Pap. Ghôran*, i.   [5] *Pap. Ghôran*, ii.
[6] ll. 128-34:

ἀνδρειοτέρους, νὴ τὴν Ἀθηνᾶν, νενόμικα
ὅσοι δύνανται τοῖς φίλοις ἀντιβλέπειν
ἀδικοῦντες ἢ τοὺς τοῖς πολεμίοις μαχομένους.
τοῖς μέν γε κοινὸς ὁ φόβος ἐστί, καὶ καλὸν
ὑπολαμβάνουσι πρᾶγμα ποιεῖν ἑκάτεροι.
τούτοις δ' ὅπως ποτ' ἐπιτρέπει τὸ συνειδέναι
αὐτοῖσι θαρρεῖν, πολλάκις τεθαύμακα.

[7] *Oxyrh. Pap.* i. 11.   [8] *Pap. Argent.* 33.
[9] *Pap. Ghôran*, ii.

three quotations, one from Philemon's $\Lambda\iota\theta o\gamma\lambda\dot{\upsilon}\phi os$, otherwise unknown, and one each from the $"H\rho\omega\epsilon s$ and $'I\kappa\dot{\alpha}\rho\iota o\iota$ of Timocles.[1]

All these fragments are printed in O. Schroeder's *Novae Comoediae Fragmenta in Papyris reperta, exceptis Menandreis,* Lietzmann's *Kleine Texte,* No. 135 (1915).   T. W. L.

---

[1] *Pap. Berol.* 9780.

I V

CALLIMACHUS

SOME twelve hundred years after his own times and within about a thousand of ours it appears that there still existed of the poems of Callimachus, besides the Epigrams, a select Corpus consisting of the six Hymns, the *Hecale*, the four books of the Αἴτια, the *Ibis*, and an abstruse poem on Athena. But almost the whole of this selection subsequently disappeared —it is presumed some time in the thirteenth century—so that until the last few years before 1900 the poetical achievement of one of the most prolific and influential *littérateurs* of Greek antiquity was represented by the six Hymns, some sixty Epigrams, and the discontinuous fragments collected from ancient citations by the acumen or industry of modern scholarship. Since 1893 the injury of fortune has in some degree been repaired by the discovery and publication[1] of substantial portions of the Αἴτια, *Hecale*, Ἴαμβοι, Μέλη, and an unidentified poem in Trochaic Tetrameters, all found in Egypt and now preserved mainly in Oxford, Vienna, Berlin, and Geneva ; there exists, in addition, some still unpublished material from Papyri.

On the basis of this extended acquaintance it is possible to frame an estimate of the poetical powers of Callimachus, not indeed essentially different, but more nicely just and on the whole more favourable than that formed by balancing the

---

[1] Αἴτια: *Oxyrh. Pap.* vii. 1011 ; xi. 1362 ; *Sitzungsb. Berl. Ak.* (1912), p. 544 ; (1914) p. 222 ; *Rev. Ét. gr.* 17, p. 216 ; *P. Ryl.* 13. Ἴαμβοι : *Oxyrh. Pap.* vii. 1011 ; xi. 1363. *Hecale* : *Mitt. Erzherz. Rainer*, vi (1897) ; *P.S.I.* ii. 133 ; (?) *Berl. Klass. Texte*, v (ii) 4 ; cf. l. 4 with Fr. 289. Μέλη : *Sitzungsb. Berl. Ak.* (1912), p. 524. Other poems : *Oxyrh. Pap.* vii. 1011 (troch. tetram.).

heavy and embroidered manner of the Hymns against the sweet but unsustained music of the Epigrams, and modified by the consideration of a few hundred disconnected lines usually distinguished by some oddity. The Hymns are now seen to be not altogether typical manifestations of Callimachus's genius; his range, which had hitherto largely to be presumed, is more plainly revealed; and though the new pieces do frequently exhibit the same precious allusiveness and sometimes rather artless pedantry, which belong both to the poet and the period, these are here more often relieved by a quizzical fancy and a pleasant lightness of hand. Above all it is impossible to withhold admiration from the power and ease of the writing. At his best Callimachus has the lesser poetical gifts in a pre-eminent degree, wit, invention, and an extraordinary dexterity in the handling of his medium, and these come to their own in the new pieces, where they are neither oppressed by the formality of the Hymn nor cramped—though this was a smaller disadvantage—by the narrow confines of the Epigram. In fact they support the view which some critics have held, that Callimachus's power lay in telling a story with artistic ease and charm, and that he was seen at his best in the Λουτρὰ Παλλάδος.

The most important in every respect of the new fragments are those of the Αἴτια, a poem in four books, concerned with the 'Origins' of various particularities of local ritual. It was long ago deduced with probability that the exordium confessed Callimachus a follower of Hesiod, that is, in the main, the Hesiod of the Catalogue; and at the end of the fourth book, now fortunately regained, Zeus seems to be introduced touching the poet's tingling ears for his loyalty and success in that discipleship. It is indeed probable that the words, 'by the hoof-print of the fiery horse',[1] are verbally repeated from the beginning to emphasize the rounded completion of the task.

That Callimachus did not cramp himself by a too close adherence to the mere essentials of the legend which he was

---

[1] *Oxyrh. Pap.* 1011, l. 86 = Front. *Ep. ad Marc.* i. 2 παρ' ἴχνιον ὀξέος ἵππου.

treating is shown by the elaboration of detail and allusion displayed in the story (from the third book) of Acontius and
Cydippe, perhaps the most famous single incident in the
whole *Αἴτια*, the concluding portion of which is contained in
Oxyrh. Pap. 1011, ll. 1–54. We possess a summary of the
story in Aristaenetus, *Epist.* i. 10, who often paraphrases the
actual language of the poem :

'Next dawn the oxen were to agonize seeing the keen
knife reflected in the water,[1] but on the eve Cydippe was
seized by a dread pallor, seized by the malady which we
conjure away on the wild goats and call by a false name sacred ;
this then grievously wasted the maiden to death's door.[2]
A second time the couches were being got ready, a second time
the girl lay ill for seven months of a quartan fever. The third
time they had thoughts of marriage, again the third time
a deadly shivering took hold on Cydippe. For a fourth time
her father tarried not, but set off to Delphi to Apollo, who in
the night uttered this word :
"A solemn oath by Artemis breaks off thy daughter's marriage, for neither was my sister harrying Lygdamis,[3] nor
plaiting rushes about Amyclae, nor washing away the soilure of
the hunt in Parthenius's stream, but was present in Delos at
that time, when thy child swore to have Acontius and none
other to her spouse. But if thou wilt take me for counsellor,
thou wilt perform thy daughter's pledge to the full. For I say
that thou wilt alloy not lead with silver in Acontius, but
electrum with bright gold . . ."' [4]

So far we have Callimachus at his best. But after a few
more lines he leaves the legend in order to give his authority,
Xenomedes, a historian of Ceos, and in twenty-four skilful
verses recounts the chief facts in the island's history mentioned
by his predecessor. Such wholesale versification reads almost
like a burlesque of poetry. A similar but much shorter statement of sources seems to be contained in *P. Ryl.* 13, ll. 5–8,

---

[1] Professor Housman has given the meaning rightly: *Class. Quart.*
iv. 115. Cf. Ov. *Fast.* i. 327 'quia praevisos in aqua timet hostia cultros' :
see also *Metam.* xv. 134.
[2] Ἀΐδεω . . . δόμων Housman : α . . εω . . . δομων Pap.
[3] Λύγδαμιν οὐ γὰρ ἐμὴ τῆμος ἔκηδε κάσις Platt : τηνον Pap.
[4] ll. 10–31.

which tells the story of Linus. It would appear that 'I sing
nothing without authority' (ἀμάρτυρον οὐδὲν ἀείδω, Fr. 442) is
a general statement of policy.[1]

In *Oxyrh. Pap.* xi. 1362, Callimachus's fresh handling of the
familiar details of a Symposion is well displayed. The
Papyrus breaks off just as the *Αἴτιον* is to begin ; but it is
worth noticing as the only extant example of Callimachus's
method of introducing his subject :

'Nor did he miss the morning when the casks are opened,
nor when Orestes' Feast of Jars brings the lucky day for slaves ;
and in celebration of the yearly rite of Icarius's child—thy day,
Erigone, so mourned by Attic women—he bade his fellows to
a feast, and among them a foreigner, newly sojourning in
Egypt, having come on some matter of his own. He was by
birth of Icus and I shared his couch, not by design, but the
saying of Homer is true, that God brings ever like to like ; for
he too abhorred to drain Thracian bumpers, and delighted in
a modest bowl. To him said I, as the goblet went round the
third time, having learnt his name and race : "Verily the
word is true that says 'wine would have not only its share of
water, but also of talk'. This let us, since it is not borne
round in ladles . . . ourselves cast as an antidote into the
dangerous draught, and do thou answer me all that I am fain
to hear from thy lips. Why is it thy country's rite to worship
Peleus, king of Myrmidons ? What has Thessaly to do with
Icus . . . ? "' (ll. 1–24).

Other fragments relating to the Return of the Argonauts[2]
(from the second book) and to the story of Heracles and
Theiodamas[3] are too disconnected for translation. We
can, however, make out from the mutilated lines of the
latter fragment that Heracles, carrying in his arms his little
son Hyllus, who has pricked his foot with a thorn, meets

---

[1] Here the reference to Xenomedes is valuable because it disposes of
the theory put forward by Mahaffy, *Greek Life and Thought*, pp. 254 sqq.,
that the Acontius-Cydippe story must have had an Oriental or, more
exactly, a Persian origin. The 'new vein of sentiment' was not 'im-
ported'; all that Callimachus did was to rescue an indigenous folk-story
from the obscurity of a local history and to treat it with such effect that
for subsequent ages it ranked as the love-romance *par excellence.—Edd.*

[2] *Rev. Ét. gr.* 17, p. 216; *Sitzungsb. Berl. Akad.* (1912), p. 544.

[3] *Sitzungsb. Berl. Akad.* (1914), p. 232.

ploughing in the field a hale old man named Theiodamas, of
whom he asks a morsel of food, for the child is hungry ; but
Theiodamas with a boorish laugh refuses.[1]   Thereupon
Heracles takes, kills, and roasts the oxen whole, disregarding
the imprecations and abuse showered upon him by Theiodamas.
The story gives the Ἀἴτιον of a sacrifice of a whole ox to
Heracles, possibly at Lindus, to the accompaniment of impre-
cations.

As a point of style, it is worth while to draw attention to the
way in which Callimachus avoids monotony in his narration
by sometimes telling the story himself, sometimes putting it
into his chief character's mouth, sometimes, by a modification
of the first method, apostrophizing his chief character as if he
were being told the story of his own deeds.[2]

Only less famous in antiquity than the Ἀἴτια was the little
epic called *Hecale* after the poor but hospitable old woman
who gave Theseus a night's lodging on his way to fight the
Marathonian bull, and upon whose funeral he came as he
returned with the captive monster.   In the Florence fragment
Theseus is recounting his mission ; in col. i of the Vienna
tablet he is returning with the huge bull, and at first inspires
great terror in the country-side.   Unfortunately the bearing of
cols. ii–iv is still very obscure, the more so as it is questioned
whether the column which stands first in the tablet does not
really continue col. iv.   All that seems clear is that a crow is
telling somebody else, who may be either a bird or a human
being, but is certainly a female, the story of Erichthonius and
the daughters of Cecrops,[3] and prophesying (with a parody
of Homer) the punishment that shall overtake the prying
raven.

This narrative occupies the last part of a night—it has been
suggested the night on Theseus's return journey corresponding

---

[1] Wilamowitz has ingeniously filled in the details of the scene:
Sitzungsb. Berl. Akad. (1914), pp. 228 sqq.
[2] So Wilamowitz, who compares (ibid. p. 227) the fragments A and B
with the manner adopted in a large part of the Molorchus legend.
[3] It will be remembered that the crow lost the favour of Athena for
officiously denouncing the maidens' breach of faith in opening the chest,
which contained the infant Erichthonius. See Ovid, *Met.* ii. 551–95.

to that spent in Hecale's hut on the way out—the fragment
ends with a charming description of dawn in a town : [1]

Καδδραθέτην δ' οὐ πολλὸν ἐπὶ χρόνον, αἶψα γὰρ ἦλθεν
στιβηεὶς ἄγχουρος· "Ἴτ', οὐκέτι χεῖρες ἔπαγροι
φιλητέων, ἤδη γὰρ ἐωθινὰ λύχνα φαείνει·
ἀείδει καί πού τις ἀνὴρ ὑδατηγὸς ἱμαῖον,
ἔγρει καί τιν' ἔχοντα παρὰ πλόον οἰκίον ἄξων
τετριγὼς ὑπ' ἄμαξαν, ἀνιάζουσι δὲ πυκνοὶ
δμῶοι χαλκῆες κωφώμενοι ἔνδον ἀκουήν."

'Not long did they slumber, for swift there came all rimy
a neighbour with : "Up, thieves' hands no longer seek their
prey, for now the lamps of dawn are shining out. The water-
drawer, I ween, sings his song at the well, and the axle,
creaking beneath the cart, wakes the dweller by the high road,
and everywhere the smithy slaves are anguished by the deafen-
ing din."'

This is realism at its best.

In the Ἴαμβοι a different side of Callimachus's skill appears.
In this poem Hipponax is brought up from Hades to address
a mass meeting, and in a long continuous poem, appropriately
written in Scazons, which, however, are devoid of the venom
that brought Bupalus to suicide, gives utterance to a loosely
connected series of anecdotes, apologues, and literary reflections.
Thus he begins by recounting the story of the cup left by the
Arcadian Bathycles τῷ σοφῶν ὀνηίστῳ. He is next discovered speaking of the fear and detestation inspired, as it
seems, by the critic of society, that is, such as himself. After
another gap follows a passage tracing an analogy between the
characters of certain kinds of people and of animals, which
could speak before Zeus 'struck them dumb'. Then comes
the best-preserved part of the whole poem, belonging to
a well-known literary genre, the *tenso* between the laurel and
the olive, in which each tree advances in turn arguments to
prove its own superiority. The laurel is getting the worst of
it when a third speaker, presumably a bush of some kind,
breaks in and counsels unity among the trees, but the laurel turns
savagely on it for its presumption in matching itself with
them.

---

[1] *Mitt. Erzherz. Rain.* vi (1897), col. iv. 10-16.

Finally there seems to be a discussion about metres.

The crispness of the writing has been sadly prejudiced by the fragmentary state of the Papyrus. The following lines from a speech by the olive will serve as a specimen : [1]

' Who made the laurel ? The earth and sun, like the ilex, oak, galingale, or any tree.

Who made the olive ? Pallas, whenas she strove against the Seaweed-dweller for Acte, and the snake-legged ancient judged between them. One fall is scored to the laurel.

Of the immortals, who honours the olive, who the laurel ? The laurel Apollo, Pallas her creation. There they are even, for I distinguish not between gods.

Of what manner is the laurel's fruit ? For what shall I use it ? Neither eat it, nor drink it, nor anoint thyself therewith. But the olive's has many uses. . . . A second fall I score against the laurel.

Whose leafage do suppliants hold out ? The olive's. For the third time the laurel is down.

Oh, tireless birds, how they chatter. Impudent crow, why is your beak not wearied out ?

And whose stump do the Delians guard ? The olive's, which gave Leto rest. . . . '

The Ἴαμβοι are followed in the Oxyrhynchus book by a poem in Trochaic Tetrameters of which little can be made out except that it is tragic in tone, and seems to have to do with a betrayed woman addressing Apollo.

Two fragments [2] remain to be noticed, one a poem on the death of Arsinoe, the sister and wife of Philadelphus, the other quoted by Athenaeus (xv. 668 C) under the title of Παννυχίς. These two come from the same Papyrus book, and have been assigned to the division of Callimachus's poems called Μέλη in Suidas's list. Both are in lyric metres used ' by the line ' ; the first in the metre called Ἀρχεβούλειον [3] by Hephaestion (ch. 8, Consb.), who quotes ll. 1, 5, and 43 of this very poem ; the

---

[1] *Oxyrh. Pap.* vii. 1011, ll. 260–80.

[2] *Sitzungsb. Berl. Ak.* (1912), pp. 524 sqq. This book also contained Αἴτια and *Hecale*.

[3] Callimachus uses it as follows :

$$\overset{\cup\cup}{\underset{\cup}{-}} \; - \cup\cup - \cup\cup - \vdots \; \cup\cup - \cup - -,$$

where : marks a diaeresis.

second in that called by the same authority (ch. 15, Consb.), ἀσυνάρτητον Εὐριπίδειον.[1]

There is too little of the Παννυχίς for discussion to be profitable. The poem on Arsinoe remains obscure owing to the hopeless mutilation of the first thirty-eight lines (which seem to describe news of her death coming down the Nile to Pharos) and the loss of the end. In what is preserved, Philotera, a sister of Arsinoe and dead before her, who has left Enna and the company of Demeter to visit Charis, Hephaestus's wife, in Lemnos, sees the smoke of Arsinoe's pyre, and fearing some harm for her old home, asks her hostess to ascend Athos, and tell her what is happening. Charis reassures her about her country, but breaks the news that her sister is dead and being mourned. That is all that can be certainly made out. The fragment is marked by a certain elaborate dignity, which is effectively sustained by the movement of the metre.

It has been said above that there still remain some fragments of Callimachus to be published, but it is improbable that our judgement will now need to be much altered. Enough remains to show that Callimachus was a man of his period, even when he surpasses it; with a mind well stored, ingenious, dexterous, sensitive; to crown these poetic gifts little was lacking but greatness of spirit. ANONYMOUS.

Other Elegiac Poems.

That the Elegiac metre was in Alexandrian times not confined to poems of sentiment, but was used for long narratives, we know from Callimachus's *Bath of Pallas*, and his *Αἴτια*. There is another instance in a fragment of seventeen lines lately discovered,[2] which treats of some incident connected with the invasion of the Gauls, which, as we have seen,[3] found its way into the poetry of the time. We can only guess at the situation. A king is threatening to punish some rebels, the news of whose defection has just been brought to him.

---

[1] Callimachus uses it as follows :

$$\bar{\cup} - \cup - \bar{\cup} - \cup -$$
$$- \cup - \cup - \cup.$$

[2] *Sitzungsb. preuss. Akad.,* 1918, p. 736.

[3] See Lyric Poetry ; Limenius, and the Anonymous Delphian Hymn.

Possibly he is an Attalid king, and we may be allowed the provisional conjecture [1] that the author may have been Musaeus of Ephesus, since Suidas states that he wrote poems in praise of Eumenes and Attalus.

Another Papyrus [2] gives an account of the simple life in the Golden Age. The language bears the stamp of the Alexandrian age, and we may compare the numerous references to the simple life in Leonidas of Tarentum, the poor man's poet.

To these we may add several new Epigrams of this age. Two are by Posidippus,[3] many of whose Epigrams are contained in the Anthology. One is on the celebrated Pharos erected in 282–281 B.C. by Sostratus of Cnidus, the great architect of the day.

The other is on the temple of Arsinoe-Aphrodite on the promontory of Zephyrium, dedicated by Callicrates, Nauarchus of the fleet in the reign of Ptolemy Philadelphus.

A Papyrus [4] of the third century B.C. gives a portion of an Epigram by a contemporary writer on the death of Philicus, who was one of the Alexandrian ' Tragic Pleiad '.

$$\dot{\epsilon}\kappa \ \kappa\iota\sigma\sigma\eta\rho\epsilon\phi\dot{\epsilon}o\varsigma \ \kappa\epsilon\phi\alpha\lambda\hat{\eta}\varsigma \ \epsilon\ddot{\upsilon}\upsilon\mu\nu\alpha \ \kappa\upsilon\lambda\dot{\iota}\omega\nu$$
$$\dot{\rho}\dot{\eta}\mu\alpha\tau\alpha \ \kappa\alpha\dot{\iota} \ \mathrm{N}\dot{\eta}\sigma\sigma\upsilon\varsigma \ \kappa\dot{\omega}\mu\alpha\sigma\sigma\nu \ \epsilon\dot{\iota}\varsigma \ \mathrm{M}\alpha\kappa\dot{\alpha}\rho\omega\nu$$

He was, says the writer, descended from Alcinous, and therefore, like a Phaeacian, knew 'how to live' $\epsilon\dot{\upsilon}\dot{\epsilon}\sigma\tau\iota\sigma\nu$. This Epigram shows that the form Philicus, which Hephaestion gives, is correct, and not Philiscus.

Two interesting Epigrams are preserved in the large and important collection of Papyri known as ' The Archives of Zenon ',[5] which belong to the middle of the third century B.C. Zenon was the agent of Apollonius, the Finance Minister of

---

[1] *Classical Rev.*, 1919, p. 90.
[2] *Oxyrh. Pap.* i, No. 14.
[3] P. Schott, *Poseidippi Epigrammata*, Nos. 1, 2.
[4] Wilamowitz, in *Neues von Kallimachos*; *Sitzungsb. Berl. Akad.*, 1912, 547.
[5] C. C. Edgar, *Selected Papyri from the Archives of Zeno; Annales du Service des Antiquités de l'Égypte*, t. xix, pp. 101 ff., H. Idris Bell; Bibliography, Graeco-Roman Egypt, A. Papyri (1915-19), in *The Journal of Egyptian Archaeology*, vol. vi, pt. ii, April 1920.

Ptolemy Philadelphus and Ptolemy Euergetes, and was employed on various commissions in Palestine, on the Red Sea, and elsewhere, finally being sent to the Fayûm to superintend the work on a great estate which had been given to Apollonius by the king. While he was hunting or travelling in the Fayum, accompanied by an Indian hound called Tauron, he encountered a wild boar. The hound attacked the boar so courageously that, although gored through the breast, he killed the boar before succumbing to his wounds, Ἰνδὸς ὡς νόμος. The hound's exploit is described in true tragic style:

κάπρῳ γὰρ ὡς συνῆλθεν ἀντίαν ἔριν,
ὁ μέν τις ὡς ἄπλατος οἰδήσας γένυν
στῆθος κατηλόκιζε λευκαίνων ἀφρῷ·
ὁ δ' ἀμφὶ νώτῳ δισσὸν ἐμβαλὼν ἴχνος
ἐδράξατο φρίσσοντος ἐκ στέρνων μέσων,
καὶ γᾷ συνεσπείρασεν.

Zenon then applied to a poet for an epitaph which he could inscribe on the hound's tombstone in memory of the brave deed. The poet sends him two, one in Elegiacs, the other in Tragic Iambics. The poet's name is not given, and the incident is not referred to in the collection of letters, although Zenon's hounds are mentioned; but the date cannot be far from 250 B.C., whether before or after. Mr. Edgar thinks it likely that ' these elaborate verses are the work of some professional man of letters in Alexandria : and no doubt more than one of the poets who clustered round the court would have been glad to do a service for a friend of the διοικητής'.[1]

An Epigram on Agesilaus is preserved on an Ostrakon now exhibited in a Bodleian show-case.[2] It is in a good style, and probably belongs to the early Ptolemaic age. It appears to have been a boy's writing-exercise, and was used for that purpose on account of the plucky words put into the lame king's mouth,

ἴξομαι, οὐδ' ἄχρειον ἐφόλκιον ἴξομαι.[3]

---

[1] The MS. is thought to be almost certainly the poet's autograph.
[2] No. 16.
[3] *Journal of Egyptian Archaeology*, v, pt. i, p. 18, Professor Grenfell's brilliant restoration. For reference to other new Epigrams see *Classical Review*, vol. xxxii, pp. 186, 187; xxxiii, p. 36; xxxiv, p. 55.

Epyllia.

The Papyri also afford us some fragments of that peculiar product of the Alexandrian school, the Epyllion. The first contains an incident in the story of Diomede.[1] The author is unknown, but the poem was known to Eustathius (on *Il. Γ.* 39), or to one of his authorities, for he illustrates the word Δύσπαρις by Αἰνόπαρις (Alcman, 40, Eur. *Hec.* 944) and by the similar formation Αἰνελένη, which occurs in the fragment, saying that ἕτερός τις used it. It is Eustathius's way to be incomplete and careless in his method of quotation.[2] This ἕτερός τις is clearly the author of our poem.

The language points to an early Hellenistic age; the style is clear and simple, and the narration rapid, as is always the case in Epyllia.[3] That the poem was of some consideration may be inferred from the manuscript. It formed part of a fine Papyrus codex of the fourth century, is written carefully, and has accents, punctuation, and metrical signs.

The scene is laid at a farm on the estate of Diomede at Argos. A trusty servant, Pheidon, son of Arcesius, is guarding the possessions of Diomede and his little son, when another trusty servant, the son of one Iphis, brings in the bad news that Argos is in the enemy's hands, and that his comrades are the prey of dogs and vultures. Pheidon is alarmed for the safety of his young charge.

A homely country scene is presented vividly. Pheidon is sitting before the door, sewing a skin together to make a winter coat, with his hounds around him. The poet gives the hounds' pedigree at length, and describes the friendly welcome which they gave him οὐρῇσιν σαίνοντες. Pheidon in alarm brings the messenger in, and shuts the door, and they begin to cast round for help.

The poem appears to bear some relation to the *Alcmaeonis*, one of the Cyclic Poems. Ephorus[4] mentions such a capture of Argos by Agamemnon in the absence of Diomede's men

---

[1] *Berl. Klass. Texte*, v. 1. 68 sqq.
[2] Pearson, *Soph. Frag.*, vol. i. lxvi.
[3] Comp. the Epyllion of Aristaeus in the Fourth Georgic.
[4] Strabo, x. 462.

with Diomede and Alcmaeon on an expedition in Aetolia and
Acarnania. But the style and language point to a date later
than the *Alcmaeonis*, and to the conclusion that an early
Hellenistic author has taken an episode from the Cyclic
Epic, just as the Epyllion of Heracles and Augeas in Theocritus xxv probably goes back to an old *Heraclea*. The loss
of the poem is regrettable.

The second is concerned with Telephus,[1] whose wife, Asty-
oche, is the speaker ; but the connexion of the ideas and the
general drift is uncertain, and the Papyrus may perhaps
contain parts of two poems. It appears from the style to be
later than the Epyllion on Diomede, and it may even be not
earlier than the date of the Papyrus itself, namely, the third
century.

Traces of a third narrative poem appear in what seems to
be a collection of Hymns of the Alexandrian age.[2] Although
the lines of the concluding poem are very fragmentary, it
evidently dealt with the story of Perseus and Andromeda, and
from some expressions in it we may conjecture that it was
known to Manilius and used by him in his Epyllion on that
subject at the end of his fifth book.

To make the list of Epyllia complete, two new fragments [3] of
Euphorion may be added ; they are the longest pieces of
Euphorion which we possess.

The first is an over-written description of Cerberus, giving
the episode of Heracles fetching him up from Hades.

The second contains a list of imprecations upon an unknown
person drawn from obscure mythology : may he have the fate
of the inquisitive Herse, Cecrops's daughter, who opened
Athena's holy chest, or of the travellers whom Sciron threw
from the rocks of the Megarid to be eaten by the tortoise, till
Theseus treated him the same way, so that he was the last to
fatten it : or may he roll Ascalaphus's stone in Hades.

In spite of some difficulties, it seems on the whole likely

[1] *Oxyrh. Pap.* ii, No. 214.
[2] The Papyrus is in the University Library of Chicago, and a new
collation of it appears in the *Journal of Philology*, xxxiv. 106 sqq.
[3] *Berl. Klass. Texte*, v. 1. 57 sqq.; Scheidweiler, *Euphorion*, Frags.
62, 95.

that the lines form part of a poem of Euphorion's already known, entitled Ἀραὶ ἢ Ποτηριοκλέπτης, in which the poet invokes curses on some one who has stolen a cup.

The lines illustrate the Alexandrian love of recondite mythology, and in particular Euphorion's artificial, laboured, and crabbed style.　He is an inferior Callimachus.

J. U. P.

V

THE MIMIAMBI OF HERONDAS

In this country the publication of Aristotle's *Constitution of Athens* quite overshadowed a work of a very different kind, which with astonishing industry Sir Frederic Kenyon gave to the world soon after that treatise in 1892 with a facsimile of the Papyrus in which it was contained. But the value of this strong light on provincial Greek life of the third century B. C. was at once seen in Germany. The veteran Bücheler promptly produced an edition with a Latin translation, which showed his matchless ingenuity and learning; Wilamowitz and Blass gave their close attention to the restoration of the text where it was fragmentary; Crusius and R. Meister dealt with its dialectical and grammatical peculiarities. In England little attention has been given to the work since the appearance of Dr. Nairn's elaborate edition and Mr. Sharpley's translation entitled *A Realist of the Aegean.*

In Herondas we have an ancient realist of the most unflinching kind. He gives us photographic pictures of common life, particularly in its least savoury aspects. He neither condemns nor approves. The honest wife, who resists the temptation of an old go-between, is to him just on the same level as the women who chatter about their vicious practices. He passes everything equally under review, the naughty schoolboy being whipped, the wily shoemaker offering his wares to extravagant women, the tax-collectors on the watch to see what customers enter a shop-door, the seamy side of slave-life. In him there is nothing of heroism, or ideal virtue, or high patriotism. Life passes before his keen eye in the busy Ionian towns, and anything will provide him with a subject.

But before dealing with his 'Scenes from daily life', we must inquire who and what he was. His name was known to us already by some thirteen fragments, chiefly preserved by Athenaeus and Stobaeus, and some of these [1] were found in the Papyrus, thus proving the authorship beyond a doubt. It is interesting to find that Eustathius attributes one quotation from Herondas to the sixth-century Ionic satirist Hipponax, of whom Herondas himself declares himself an imitator and follower.[2] Both sang to the 'sons of Xuthus', i. e. the Ionians ; both may have lived in the same town. Athenaeus alone calls our author Herondas : others gave his name as Herodas. The name Herodas was common enough, but we should hardly expect a writer who uses the Ionic dialect to be called Herondas, a form best known to us from Boeotia, if that had not been his real name. Probably he called himself Herondes, as he speaks of the Catanaean legislator as Chaerondes. It is of course possible that, as Dr. Nairn thinks, Herondas is a corruption of Heroidas ; but it is more probable that Herondas was to the common name Heron, as Philondas to Philon, or Epameinondas to Epameinon.

The dialect of the Papyrus is a conventional literary Ionic, with few—surprisingly few—Doricisms, and a good many Attic forms. Most of the latter must simply be due to copyists ; it is not conceivable that the author wrote indifferently κοῖος and ποῖος, γλῶσσα and γλᾶσσα. The vocabulary is popular throughout, and teems with picturesque and proverbial phraseology, with hardly any poetical flavour, though occasionally there is a touch of it, as when the women of Egypt are said to be more in number than the stars, γυναῖκες ὁκόσους . . . ἀστέρας ἐνεγκεῖν οὐρανὸς κεκαύχηται.

Herondas then aimed at being the poet of the Ionians like Hipponax. His name however would seem to imply that he belonged to the southern Sporades, and the internal evidence of the poems confirms this conjecture. We are confined to internal evidence for his date, which is certain within narrow limits. In the first scene we are introduced to a woman whose husband has gone off to Egypt. Among the glories of that country is 'the sacred precinct of the divine brother and sister' (θεῶν ἀδελφῶν τέμενος, l. 30). Plainly then this

---

[1] i. 15, 67 ; vi. 37.   [2] Hipp., Fr. 75 (Bergk) ; ix. 10.

poem was written after the death of Arsinoe, which took
place between May and July 270 B. C., and the institution by
Philadelphus of a cult of himself and his departed consort.
Next is mentioned the ' King good and kind ', i. 30, and it
was natural at first to think of Ptolemy Euergetes, who came
to the throne in 246 B. C. If it referred to him, the date of
the poem would probably fall before the defeat of Euergetes
at Andros in 242 B. C., when he lost the Cyclades. But
scholars are now inclined to refer it to Philadelphus, as the
King in his active capacity can easily be differentiated from
the same king as one of the divine pair. If Philadelphus is
intended, the lower limit for the poem would be the battle
of Cos in 253 B. C., when he temporarily lost control of the
Aegean to Antigonus. Now the fourth poem of Herondas
irresistibly reminds us of Theocritus's fifteenth Idyll, ' The
Woman at the Feast of Adonis ', and there are also points of
contact between Herondas's second poem and the fourteenth
Idyll of Theocritus, which is not far distant in date from the
fifteenth. Dr. Nairn has made it probable that Herondas was
the imitator and not vice versa. Theocritus's hexameter dealing with everyday life had been a success, and our author,
who was apparently a member of the literary circle which had
a meeting-place in Cos, took the hint for his dramatic scenes.

This leads us to a consideration of the title *Mimiambi*.
They are written in the limping ' senarii ', called Scazons by
the Greeks, perhaps invented, certainly first made popular by
Hipponax. Were they written only to be read, or to be
actually produced ? Any one who reads Herondas will
assuredly feel a conviction that they were intended for
dramatic production. The founders of the Mime, Epicharmus
and Sophron, must have set that fashion, and one's irresistible
impression is that this author too wrote for a stage. It is
more difficult to decide whether they were rendered by a
single actor or in parts, and the answer to that question
cannot be so positive. On the whole the difficulty of actually staging the beginning of the first and the whole of the
fourth poem is slightly in favour of the hypothesis of a
single actor. The sallies against women were quite in the

conventional line of Ionic satire (Semonides of Amorgos and Hipponax), and must have been sure of applause.

The Papyrus gives us 7co lines more or less complete and capable of restoration, and about 180 more in which no great certainty as to the filling of the lacunae is possible. There are seven complete pieces: (1)'The Lena'; (2) 'The Leno'; (3) 'The Schoolmaster'; (4) 'The Women at the Temple of Asclepius' ; (5) 'The Jealous Woman'; (6) 'Women in Private Conversation' ; (7) 'The Shoemaker.' The eighth gives a ' Dream ' told by a mistress to a slave, the details of which can hardly be restored. With this apparently the first book came to an end, and of the second book we have the title and a few fragments of ' Women at Breakfast ', Ἀπονηστιζόμεναι, to which the previously known fragments add two more titles, 'Women working together', Συνεργαζόμεναι, and 'The Musician', Μολπεινός.

The scene of the second and fourth pieces is Cos: the probabilities are in favour of a Coan setting for the first and third. If in V. 80 Dr. Walter Headlam's ingenious conjecture Ἀγριήνια for the unknown feast Γερήνια of the Papyrus be adopted, the fifth is also Coan, as the calendar of Cos had a month Agrianius. In the sixth piece there are no secure indications. The ubiquity of the τελῶναι, who watch every door, might suggest Alexandria, but dues on goods sold were collected in many places and might have been so in Cos. A more important point is that the names of the women occur in identical or almost identical forms in Coan inscriptions. Thus in Paton and Hicks's *Corpus* we find Corittas, Nossis, and Bitias in inscriptions of 230 B.C. or thereabouts. But the scene of the seventh poem, ' The Shoemaker's Shop ', cannot be Cos, as Taureôn (l. 86) is not a Coan month and probably points to Ephesus. Dr. Rutherford inferred from the proper name Artakene that the scene was laid at Cyzicus, but the name, even if derived from Artake, may quite well have been formed elsewhere. Cos was then a very flourishing free πόλις, valuing its independence [1] and proud of its school of medicine and astronomy,[2] and doubtless also of the coterie of poets

[1] ii. 26.   [2] iii. 54.

which had gathered round Philetas. It was certainly in close connexion with Egypt, as is shown by not only the first piece but the fourteenth Idyll of Theocritus, the scene of which must be laid in Cos. 'Only in Cos', as Mr. Cholmeley remarks, 'can we find a reasonable meeting-place for a philosopher from Athens, an Argive, and a Pharsalian horse-dealer.' In the narrow alleys (λαῦραι) of this seaport town mud was up to the knee;[1] skippers of coasting ships put in and behaved in no very reputable fashion; husbands left their wives to seek their fortunes in Egypt;[2] all manner of artisans advertised their wares 'such as Athene herself might have produced';[3] the schoolmasters beat truants,[4] and slaves were either sent to the brander[5] (στίκτης) or the regular place of punishment (ζήτρειον, mentioned for Chios by the *Etymologicum Magnum*). It was above all the life of the women that our author liked to depict. Naturally their relations with their domestics occupy a good deal of their conversation. The offending slave is 'a stone, not a handmaid', 'a robber', 'a gormandizer'; they sleep the 'sleep of Endymion', they are 'ears and tongues, mind-stuffers and nothing but holiday-makers'; they count the grains of their food allowance, and if any drop, they go about grumbling and fuming the whole day. There is a darker side to slave life in Scene V, where a jealous mistress who has had a liaison with a slave detects him with a fellow slave and first orders him to be beaten to death, then changes her mind and fetches him back to be branded, but yields to the intercession of a favourite slave-girl and gives him a reprieve.

The second scene is a speech in a law-court, delivered by a pander, who claims damages for assault and abduction of one of his women from a ship's captain. It is obviously a parody of Attic forensic speeches, such as that of Hypereides for Phryne. The impudence of the fellow is to the life, and his λοιδορία of his opponent most realistic. 'He was once a Phrygian called Artemnes, now he pretends to be a Greek and calls himself Thales.' 'These outrages he committed

[1] i. 14.   [2] i. 23.   [3] vi. 65; vii. 116.
[4] iii. 77.   [5] v. 28, 32.

and has no respect for law or προστάτης or magistrate' (the officials called Prytaneis at Athens were called Prostatai at Cos). 'One day you live at Bricindera (a township in Rhodes), the next at Abdera; to-morrow, if any one will pay your fare, you will be off to Phaselis', the inhabitants of which place had no very good reputation according to the pseudo-Demosthenes' speech 'Against Lacritus'. Finally he winds up with an appeal to the legendary glories of Cos, Merops, Heracles, and Thessalus,[1] and to Asclepius, whose sanctuary was the chief pride of the island, and winds up with the effective quotation of the proverb Φρὺξ ἀνὴρ πληγεὶς ἀμείνων.

Comparable to the impudence of the 'Leno' is the mixture of flattery and abuse with which the shoemaker, Cerdo, exhibits his wares in piece VII. He gets apparently most exorbitant prices out of the spendthrift women, and then promises a pair of 'crab'-shoes as commission to the lady who introduced them. Great pains are taken to make the language appropriate to characters. Thus the shoemaker swears 'by the heart of Cerdo' and 'by my bald temple'; the faithful wife 'by the home-coming of my husband and dear Demeter', or 'by the Fates'; the schoolboy 'by the dear Muses', whom he has so shamefully neglected; the angry mistress 'by the queen' (Hera or Aphrodite); the gossiping women 'by these sweet (eyes)'. Here we have obviously a transcript from the language of daily life. Herondas has added to the proverbial stock of the Greek language. 'He has drunk of a new (cup)' (πέπωκεν ἐκ καινῆς), says the temptress to the forsaken wife, and 'a ship is not safe riding at one anchor' (νηῦς μιῆς ἐπ' ἀγκύρης οὐκ ἀσφαλὴς ὁρμοῦσα): the latter replies, 'If anybody else had talked to me like that, I'd have taught her to go limping away for her lame advice' (χωλὴν ἀείδειν χωλά). 'Looking at me with eyes bigger than a crab' (καρκίνου μέζον ὁρεῦσα); 'giggling louder than a mare whinnies' (μέζον ἵππου κιχλίζουσα); 'washing your tongue in honey'; 'paying principal and interest' (of increased punishment); 'having your bile on your nose-tip' (i. e. always ready to fly in a passion); 'straining out of a perforated (vessel)' (ἐκ τετρημένης ἠθεῖν), of stops

[1] *Iliad* B 679.

between every word in recitation ; ' as like as two figs ' (where
we say ' peas '), are specimens of these expressive sayings,
some of which are more obscure, e. g. ' to weep like Nannacus '
(it is an odd coincidence that this is a Coan name [1]) ; or ' the
moon of Acesaeus ', which is said elsewhere to refer to pro-
crastination. ' One who does not even move a chip from the
ground ' (οὐδὲ κάρφος ἐκ τῆς γῆς κινέων), of a quiet and sober
person, comes in Aristophanes.

The fourth scene gives us the gossip of two women, Coccale
and Cynno, who are bringing an offering of a cock and a votive
tablet to the Asclepieion, apologizing for being poor and
unable to offer an ox or a pig.   The chief interest of the piece
is that they admire the votive offerings first outside the temple.
There is a work by the sons of Praxiteles, who are apparently
still alive, as they remark ' May Paean be gracious to them ' :
this is strongly in favour of a date as near to 270 B. C. as
possible.   Other works of art mentioned are a maiden looking
at an apple, an old woman, a boy strangling a fox-goose,
which suggests the work of Boethus,[2] and a portrait-statue of
a woman.   When the sacristan arrives and opens the temple
door, they join the jostling crowd and get inside, where they
admire the paintings by Apelles, who ended his life at Cos,
apparently of a sacrificial procession, a boy with the inward
parts and tongs (σπλαγχνόπτης), an ox, the man leading it
with an attendant woman, a hook-nosed man and a shock-
headed one.   Then comes what is clearly a defence of Apelles
against hostile criticism.   ' No one can say " this man saw one
thing and failed at another ", but whatever god he conceived
a design of touching, he set to work ; and may any one who
has seen him or his works without justly admiring them, be
hung up by the post in the house of the fuller ' and tortured !

Probably the best-known piece is ' The Schoolmaster '.   An
infuriated mother brings the truant to the schoolmaster to be
beaten.   He will not go to school, but, tired of playing with
bumble-bees, he now goes off to play ' chuck-farthing ' with
low characters like porters and runaway slaves.   He won't try
to get on with his reading, even when his old father helps him,

[1] Paton and Hicks, 160.   [2] Pliny, *Nat. Hist.* xxxiv. 84.

and so she has to pay the school-fees for nothing : she might as well set him to feed donkeys. If scolded, he either runs away to his grandmother or climbs on the roof and squats there like a monkey, breaking tiles, which have to be paid for at an obol and a half apiece, before the bad weather sets in. All the neighbours put down any mischief to Metrotime's Kottalos. The schoolmaster vows to reduce him to order. The boy pleads : (iii. 71 sqq.)

Κότταλος. Μὴ μὴ ἱκετεύω, Λαμπρίσκε, πρός σε τῶν Μουσέων
καὶ τοῦ γενείου τῆς τε Κουτίδος ψυχῆς,
μὴ τῷ με δριμεῖ, τῷ 'τέρῳ δὲ λώβησαι,
The master replies :
Ἀλλ' εἷς πονηρός, Κότταλε, ὥστε καὶ περνὰς
οὐδείς σ' ἐπαινέσειεν, οὐδ' ὅκως χώρης
οἱ μῦς ὁμοίως τὸν σίδηρον τρώγουσιν.
The boy still pleads :
Κόσας, κόσας, Λαμπρίσκε, λίσσομαι, μέλλεις
ἔς μευ φορῆσαι; Λα. Μὴ 'μέ, τήνδε δ' εἰρώτα·
τατᾶ. Κό. Κόσας μοι δώσετ'; Μη. Εἴ τί σοι ζώην,
φέρειν ὅσας ἂν ἡ κακὴ σθένῃ βύρσα.
Κό. Παῦσαι, ἱκαναί, Λαμπρίσκε. Λα. Καὶ σὺ δὴ παῦσαι
κάκ' ἔργα πρήσσων. Κο. Οὐκέτ', οὐχί ⟨τι⟩ πρήξω,
ὄμνυμί σοι, Λαμπρίσκε, τὰς φίλας Μούσας.
Λα. Ὅσσην δὲ καὶ τὴν γλάσσαν, οὗτος, ἔσχηκας·
πρός σοι βαλέω τὸν μῦν τάχ', ἢν πλέω γρύξῃς.
Κό. Ἰδού, σιωπῶ· μή με, λίσσομαι, κτείνῃς.
Λα. Μέθεσθε, Κόκκαλ', αὐτόν. Μη. Οὐ δεῖ σ' ἐκλῆξαι,
Λαμπρίσκε, δεῖρον δ' ἄχρις ἥλιος δύῃ.

Boy. Oh, Lampriskos, I implore you by the Muses, and by your beard, and by the life of your dear one, don't leather me with the stinger, but with the other.
Master. Nay, but you are such a rascal, Kottalos, that even if one were trying to sell you, he couldn't say any good of you, even in the land where mice eat iron as common fare.
Boy. How—how many are you going to give me ?
Master. Don't ask me, ask her. Swish, swish !
Boy. How many shall I have, mother ?
Mother. As you love me, bear as many as your ugly hide will stand.
Boy. Stop, enough, Lampriskos !
Master. Well, do *you* stop your evil ways.
Boy. I won't, I won't do it again. I swear it, Lampriskos, by the dear Muses.

Master. What a long tongue you have got! I'll stop your mouth with the gag, if you say a word more.
Boy. There, I am mum. Don't, please, kill me.
Master. Let him down, Kokkalos.
Mother. Don't stop, Lampriskos. Thrash him till sunset.

Then the boy is released, but the mother protests it is not enough. The schoolmaster, however, undertakes that he shall get twenty more in class 'though he read better than Clio herself',

ἦν μέλλῃ
αὐτῆς ἄμεινον τῆς Κλεοῦς ἀναγνῶναι.

At this point apparently the boy escapes, and the mother vows she will go home and tell the old man and come back with fetters, so that he may be chained up in school in sight of the Divine Ladies whom he hates. This is the lighter side of realism.

Not without justice has Herondas been compared by M. Théodore Reinach to Ostade or Teniers. If we had his work complete, we might find the drunken slave of Plautus, but there would be the lightness of the Greek touch. Theocritus is a poet, while Herondas is only a versifier, and a very rugged one at that, but there is a life and vigour about him which make him a worthy contemporary.   G. C. R.

APPENDIX

The later Greek Mime.

The Mimes of Sophron, Theocritus, and Herondas are definitely literary; if they were ever performed on the stage, it was before an audience of considerable culture. But the popular taste demanded something less subtle; and in Hellenistic, as in Byzantine times, there was no lack of artists prepared to supply what the public wanted. So much we were able to infer from the references in Athenaeus and similar writers, from the numerous inscriptions mentioning famous *archimimi* and *archimimae*, and especially from the repeated denunciations of pagan and Christian moralists. But the history of the popular Mime in Greece remained a difficult and

thorny subject, because, owing to the ephemeral nature of
these productions, there was little or no direct evidence. In
1903 this gap was to some extent filled by the publication
of an Oxyrhynchus Papyrus containing two pieces of this
description, one a Farce or Burlesque, the other a Mime
proper.[1] The Papyrus belongs to the second century A. D.,
but the compositions themselves are variously assigned to
late Ptolemaic or early Imperial times.

The Farce, which in Crusius's edition[2] is entitled Χαρίτιον,
and runs to some 230 lines, is a parody of the story made
famous in tragedy by Euripides' *Iphigenia in Tauris*. A Greek
maiden, Charition, is held captive by Indian barbarians : her
brother succeeds in rescuing her after making the Indians and
their king too drunk to follow in pursuit. The barbarians
are represented as speaking their own language, and this has
been identified by Orientalists as Kanarese, one of the Dravidian
languages of Southern India.[3]

Most of the piece is written in prose, but towards the end we
find a medley of metres, chiefly Sotadeans and Trochaic Tetrameters. It has been suggested that the piece, as we have it,
is really an acting edition, not intended for private reading, an
explanation which would certainly account for the abbreviated
stage-directions scattered about plentifully, and for the fact
that one scene is given in two different versions, of which one
has been more vulgarized than the other.[4] The following
lines give a good idea of the whole : Charition and her party
are leaving the temple.

(A = Charition, B = Slave, C = Brother)

B. Κυρία Χαρίτιον, ἑτοιμάζου ἐὰν δυνηθῇς τι τῶν ἀναθημά-
    των τῆς θεοῦ μαλῶσαι.[5]
A. εὐφήμει· οὐ δεῖ τοὺς σωτηρίας δεομένους μεθ' ἱεροσυλίας
    ταύτην παρὰ θεῶν αἰτεῖσθαι . . .

---

[1] *Oxyrh. Pap.* iii. 413.
[2] *Herondae Mimiambi*[5], &c., ed. Crusius, Teubner, 1914.
[3] Comp. Hultzsch, *Hermes*, 1904, 307 sqq.
[4] ll. 30–57 = ll. 188–230.
[5] Supposed to mean ' put under the arm and carry off' ; comp. μάλη.
More probably = ἀμαλῶσαι : cf. Hesych. ἀμαλλοῖ (ἀμαλοῖ M. Schmidt),
ἀφανίσαι.

B. σὺ μὴ ἅπτου· ἐγὼ ἀρῶ.
A. μὴ παῖζε, ἀλλ' ἐὰν παραγένωνται, διακόνει αὐτοῖς τὸν οἶνον
    ἄκρατον.
B. ἐὰν δὲ μὴ θέλωσιν οὕτως πίνειν ;
C. μωρέ,[1] ἐν τούτοις τοῖς τόποις οἶνος οὐκ ὤνειος . . .

The Mime is altogether a more realistic, not to say sordid, production. The piece seems to fall naturally into six or seven short scenes (187 lines in Crusius's edition ; the beginning is lost), and the action is apparently as follows :[2] The '*archimima*' plays the part of a faithless wife, who, as the play now opens, is trying to persuade Aesopus, one of her slaves and the object of her passion, to accede to her demands. Aesopus is in love with a fellow slave, Apollonia, and in spite of threats remains obdurate. His mistress in a fury orders both of the lovers to be taken off and left to die in a desolate spot. But the slaves charged with the execution of this command are not loyal to their mistress, and in Scene II they return and inform her that the prisoners (whom they have really released) have been rescued by divine intervention. The woman is only half-deceived, but she halts between suspicion and superstitious awe. However, her doubts are soon resolved, for Apollonia betrays the scheme by a premature return and is again handed over to suffer the extreme penalty, while strict orders are given for the apprehension of Aesopus (Scene III). Scene IV opens with the bringing in of the corpse of Aesopus, who the slaves pretend has thrown himself from a height. Really he has been drugged by his fellows for his own good. Confronted with the supposed corpse the mistress gives way to sentiment and laments his suicide. But she is soon consoled for her loss by another slave, Malacus, who is only too anxious to play the part declined by Aesopus. Mistress and paramour then conspire to poison their lord and master, but the other slaves again combine to defeat them, and though the old man is

---

[1] Not *Stupide*, as Crusius apparently, but an ordinary term of vulgar abuse ; comp. Matt. v. 22 ὃς δ' ἂν εἴπῃ Μωρέ, ἔνοχος ἔσται εἰς τὴν γέενναν τοῦ πυρός, and the Modern Greek βρέ = μωρέ.

[2] Some, e. g. Schubart, *Einführung in die Papyruskunde*, pp. 138-40, suppose that the remains comprise two distinct mimes. Sudhaus, *Hermes*, 1906, 247 sqq., argued for the unity of the piece. Crusius agrees with him.

brought in as dead, he soon gets up and denounces the con-
spirators, who then meet the punishment they deserve. Meanwhile the drugged Aesopus, and Apollonia, whose corpse
must also have been brought on the stage and added to his,
are found to be alive and well.   So all ends happily.

It will be seen that in the earlier portion of the piece we
have a version of the theme treated by Herondas in his fifth
Mime ; but the hurried action of the Oxyrhynchus fragment
gives no room for the psychological analysis which Herondas
attempts, and indeed the piece, as it now stands, is very obscure
in details.[1]   As in the Farce, we have probably only the outline of a play jotted down as the basis on which the company
could improvise as they pleased.   The *archimima* is all-
important.   She holds all the threads of the action in her
hands, and some have even supposed that by making plentiful
use of gesticulation, &c., she managed to act the whole piece
without assistance, but this seems improbable.   The Mime is
written in prose except for the last line: the language is the
Κοινή, but with fewer vulgarisms than might have been
expected.

Very scanty fragments of another Mime are preserved in
Pap. Londin. 1984.[2]   The remains are too meagre for us to
reconstruct the plot with any certainty ; but it is interesting to
find that the fragment is inscribed ἐκ βιβλιοθήκης Πρασίου
Ἡρακλείδης,[3] a note which, as Crusius says, suggests that
these texts were not in use among the players only, but sometimes found their way into respectable libraries.   E. A. B.

---

[1] The *résumé* given above follows generally the reconstruction of
Sudhaus.

[2] Comp. Körte, *Archiv für Papyrusforschung*, vi. 1 sqq. ; Crusius, op.
cit., pp. 117-21.

[3] Crusius supplies ἀπέγραψα.

VI

HISTORY AND BIOGRAPHY

The Oxyrhynchus Historian.

OF all the papyrological discoveries of the last thirty years few have aroused a greater interest, and none have given rise to keener controversy, than that of a fragment of a historian who has been variously identified with Ephorus, with Theopompus, and with Cratippus. As the fragment contains little more than 500 complete lines, it cannot be compared in respect of length with the *Constitution of Athens* or with the fragments of Bacchylides. Its importance, however, is not to be gauged by its length. Nor does its value lie solely in the contribution that it makes to the history of Greece in the early years of the fourth century B.C. If the view is correct which identifies the author of this fragment with Ephorus, we have before us for the first time the actual handiwork of one of the most famous historians of antiquity, one of the two most illustrious exponents of the new style of historical writing that developed under the influence of Rhetoric. For the first time we are in a position to judge of the literary art of Ephorus, of his historical method, and of his scientific value. It is hardly of less moment that the fragment enables us, for the first time, to form a just estimate of the importance of the work of Diodorus Siculus, a writer to whom we owe the sole continuous narrative that we possess of the history of Greece from the Invasion of Xerxes to the end of the fourth century B.C., but whose authority has suffered both from the late date (the reign of Augustus) at which he wrote and from the lack of literary skill that he exhibits.

The fragment, which was discovered by Grenfell and Hunt, and published by them in Part V of the *Oxyrhynchus Papyri* (No. 842), in 1907, is concerned with the events of the year 395 B.C., and possibly with some of the events of the preceding year. It narrates the first campaign of Agesilaus and the battle of Sardis, the overthrow and assassination of Tissaphernes, the revolution at Rhodes, the origin of the Boeotian War, and the mutiny of the Cypriotes in Conon's fleet. It breaks off at the end of the second campaign of Agesilaus. In addition to the events which are narrated, much incidental information is given on a number of points, such as the origin of the Corinthian War, political parties at Athens and Thebes, and the effects of the occupation of Decelea on the condition of the rural parts of Attica. It is in one of these digressions, in connexion with the outbreak of the Boeotian War, that we have the most valuable chapter of the whole fragment, the famous description of the constitution of the Boeotian League. Of the period of Greek history with which the fragment is concerned we have two other accounts—that which is contained in Book III of the *Hellenics* of Xenophon, and that which is contained in Book XIV of Diodorus. Nothing is more remarkable in the fragment than its divergences from Xenophon and its coincidences with Diodorus. In the account of the first campaign of Agesilaus and the fall of Tissaphernes the agreement with Diodorus is close, and the coincidences are verbal. It is these coincidences that afford the clue to the authorship. Of Xenophon's narrative, on the other hand, the account in the fragment appears to be wholly independent. The divergences between the two are frequent and serious. They relate to matters of such importance as the sending of the Persian gold to Argos, Thebes, and the other enemies of Sparta, which Xenophon ascribes to Tithraustes and the fragment to Timocrates (i. e. the fragment puts the Persian intrigues with the anti-Laconian party in Greece before the fall of Tissaphernes, while Xenophon puts them after it) ; the first campaign of Agesilaus and the battle of Sardis, where the two accounts differ both as to the line of march followed by Agesilaus and the details of the engagement ; the origin of the Boeotian War ; and the second campaign of Agesilaus. But the divergence from Xenophon does not end with the discrepancies between the two accounts. The difference between the two extends to the perspective of

the operations.   In the fragment the naval warfare bulks
large.   We have a detailed narrative of the revolution at
Rhodes, of the mutiny of the Cypriotes in the fleet at Caunus,
and of the activities of Conon.   The operations by sea appear
as contributing as much to the final result as the campaigns
on land ; Conon is hardly less prominent a figure than Agesilaus himself.   In Xenophon the naval warfare is passed over
in silence.   It is these divergences from Xenophon, whose
version of the events of this period had hitherto gone un-
challenged, that give rise to the question of the authority of
the fragment.

To take first the question of authority.

There is clearly much in the fragment the value of which
would be admitted by all.   The chapter on the constitution of
Boeotia is of first-rate importance.   Our knowledge of the
constitutions of the Greek states, other than Athens and
Sparta, is meagre in the extreme.   We have now for the first
time a fairly full, and fairly clear, account of the constitution
of one of the leading states.   What adds to the interest of
the chapter is that the constitution described is federal in
character.   The account, again, of the naval operations bears
upon it the stamp of authenticity.   The touches in the story
of the mutiny at Caunus, when taken in connexion with the
fullness of detail which is elsewhere apparent in this part of
the narrative, render it difficult to question the conclusion that
the author's information came, at first or second hand, from
an eyewitness.   The value of the account is open to as little
question as its authenticity.   The naval warfare, which in the
Hellenics figures as a mere incident, was clearly of more importance in determining the issue than the operations on land.
The life-like touches which are apparent in the mutiny at
Caunus can be detected both in the episode of Demaenetus and
in the digression about the devastation of Attica in the
Decelean War.   In both passages the narrative must go back
to an eyewitness.   And although in the motives for their
hostility to Sparta which he ascribes to the leading statesmen
in Thebes, Corinth, and Argos, as well as at Athens, he shows
less grasp of the political situation than Xenophon, his view of

the attitude of the two parties at Athens, the Conservatives, led by Thrasybulus and Anytus, and the Radicals, under Epicrates and Cephalus, is almost certainly just. When we come to the actual discrepancies between our author and Xenophon a decision is more difficult. In the account of the second campaign of Agesilaus, in the autumn of 395 B. C., the discrepancies relate to an episode in which Xenophon was keenly interested—that of Spithridates and Agesilaus, and of the alliance concluded between the latter and the Paphlagonian king Otys, through the influence of the former. Where the two accounts of this episode differ, Xenophon is unquestionably right and the fragment wrong. But it may well be that in the route ascribed to Agesilaus's army the fragment is correct. Xenophon affords us hardly any data as to the line of march, while in the fragment the description is detailed and the topography excellent. In the two accounts of the outbreak of the Boeotian War, which present some remarkable contrasts (e. g. the Locrians, who play an important part in both narratives, are the Opuntian in one version, the Ozolian in the other), it is far from proven that all the error is on the side of the fragment. We are dealing here, in the main, with secret designs and secret negotiations, and when the game of political intrigue is being played, different versions of what has happened are likely to obtain currency, even at the time. The War from which we have just emerged is rich in illustrations of this truth. More than one story was current as to the intrigues that led up to the outbreak of the Boeotian War—that is clear. Xenophon gives us the simpler story, and our author a more complicated one. It does not follow that the simpler version is the true. It is in the narrative of the first campaign of Agesilaus and the battle of Sardis that the presumption in favour of Xenophon is strongest. The discrepancies are nowhere graver than here. The route which seems to be indicated in Xenophon is the direct one from Ephesus to Sardis, over Mount Tmolus, while in the fragment it is indirect and much longer. In the latter, the result of the battle turns on the success of an ambush, and Tissaphernes is present; in Xenophon, Tissaphernes remains in

Sardis, and there is no ambush. On all these points it is difficult not to accept Xenophon's version. The ambush in particular, which figures again in the autumn campaign of Agesilaus, looks like a conventional touch.

There remains the question of authorship.

When the Papyrus was first discovered there were three considerations which seemed to point to Ephorus as the author of the fragment—the coincidences with Diodorus, the style, and the survival of the work to so late a date as the second century A. D. The claims of Ephorus would have been generally conceded, had it not been for two assumptions which were universally accepted, and which seemed fatal to the hypothesis that Ephorus was the author. These assumptions related to the scale of the work and the method of its composition. It was assumed that the scale of the fragment was too elaborate for the work of Ephorus, which was a universal history, covering the whole period from the return of the Heraclidae to the outbreak of the Sacred War in the fourth century B.C. It was also assumed, on the strength of a passage in Diodorus, that the method of Ephorus was not annalistic, or synchronistic, like that of the fragment, but κατὰ γένος, i. e. that Ephorus's method was to deal with a subject and to finish it off before he passed on to another, while the method of the fragment is to follow the strict chronological sequence of events, after the manner of Thucydides. As the claims of Ephorus seemed to be barred by these assumptions, it remained to find an author to whom the fragment might be ascribed. The two names that were suggested were those of Theopompus and Cratippus.

In favour of Theopompus there are two arguments. His *Hellenica* was a continuation of Thucydides. It started from the battle of Cynossema, where Thucydides breaks off, and it ended with the battle of Cnidus, in 394 B.C. The scale, therefore, of a work which covered only seventeen years seemed consistent with that of the Papyrus. And it is not improbable that the *Hellenica* should have been read in Egypt in the second century A.D., although it enjoyed much less popularity than his *Philippica*. Against Theopompus there are two arguments which may fairly be called conclusive—the style, and the relation to Diodorus. While the style of the fragment agrees with all that we are told as to the style of Ephorus—it is diffuse, tame, and dull—it is the very opposite of all that we associate with Theopompus. Beyond all question, it is the style of a writer who needed, not the bridle, but the spur.

The coincidences between Diodorus and the fragment constitute an objection not less weighty. As Diodorus derived his history from Ephorus, and not from Theopompus (this may be taken as agreed), the coincidences can only be explained by the hypothesis that Ephorus followed Theopompus so closely that the actual words and phrases of the latter historian can still be traced in Diodorus. There is neither evidence nor probability of any such use of Theopompus by Ephorus. Nor is it in the least degree more probable that Ephorus made a similar use of Cratippus, or of any other writer of the period.

The claims of Theopompus were advocated by Wilamowitz and Eduard Meyer, but not even the combined weight of these two famous names sufficed to win general acceptance for their view. Those who refuse to admit Ephorus are coming more and more to fall back on Cratippus.

Cratippus is a writer of whom we know next to nothing. Not a line of him has survived, and in the whole of ancient literature there are but four references to him. He was a contemporary, in some sense or other, of Thucydides; he completed Thucydides' work ; he carried his history down at least as far as the battle of Cnidus ; and he objected to the introduction of speeches into historical works. The absence of speeches in our fragment can hardly constitute a serious argument in favour of Cratippus. All that can be said for him is that he covered the period with which our fragment deals, and that he may have written on a scale not less elaborate. It is true that his advocates have one great advantage on their side. A writer of whom hardly anything is known is a writer of whom almost anything may be assumed. His style, e.g., *may* have been indistinguishable from that of

Ephorus, and his narrative *may* have been followed by the latter as closely as you please. These are assertions which, in the nature of the case, cannot be disproved. Against Cratippus there is the improbability that a writer who was unknown to Diodorus should have been read at Oxyrhynchus, in Egypt, a couple of centuries later. If it can be shown that the current assumptions as to the scale and method of Ephorus are unsound, the case for Cratippus disappears.

In my lectures on the *Hellenica Oxyrhynchia* I have endeavoured to disprove both these assumptions. I have shown that the scale of Ephorus's work was much more elaborate than that of the *Hellenica* of Xenophon. I proved, from an examination of Diodorus, that there was much that was omitted by Xenophon that was narrated by Ephorus, and that there were many events narrated by both that were much more fully narrated by Ephorus, e. g. the battles of Abydos, Cyzicus, and Arginusae, in the last period of the Peloponnesian War. And I endeavoured to prove, from an examination of our fragment, that the scale on which events are narrated in it is not at all inconsistent with the scale that may reasonably be ascribed to Ephorus. I endeavoured also to prove, from an examination of Book XIV of Diodorus, that the method of Ephorus, in this part of his work, corresponded precisely to the method of the fragment; i. e. that Ephorus passed from subject to subject, and from scene to scene, exactly as the fragment does, in obedience to the sequence of events. But if any one has still any lingering doubts on the subject, he need only turn to Diodorus's narrative of the Peloponnesian War. It would be too much to say that the order in Diodorus is always that which we find in Thucydides, for there are several episodes which are narrated synchronistically in Thucydides, and κατὰ γένος in Diodorus. But on the whole, there is a remarkably close correspondence between the order in Thucydides and that in Diodorus. In the first four years there is hardly a single divergence. This of itself proves that Ephorus could and did write according to the method of our fragment. Diodorus's statement [1] as to the

---

[1] Book V, ch. 1.

method of Ephorus holds good of his work down to the outbreak of the Peloponnesian War.   It does not hold good of
the later portions of his history.

When once these two assumptions as to scale and method
have been disproved, it is difficult to resist the arguments
which are founded on the coincidences with Diodorus, and on
the style.

It is one of the most certain results of historical criticism
that the *Bibliotheca Historica* of Diodorus was based, so far as
the history of Greece is concerned, on the work of Ephorus.   As
has been already pointed out, there is the closest correspondence between Diodorus's account of the first campaign of
Agesilaus and the account of the same campaign in the
Papyrus, nor are the coincidences confined to this campaign.
They are precisely such as we should expect to find if the
author of the fragment were Ephorus.   They are of the same
character as those which we find between Diodorus and a
fragment relating to the earlier part of the Pentecontaetia
which is certainly from the pen of Ephorus.[1]   If our fragment
is not by Ephorus, we are forced to assume that Ephorus
followed the author of the fragment—Theopompus, or Cratippus, or whoever he may be—as servilely and mechanically as
Diodorus followed Ephorus.   But what is credible of Diodorus is incredible of Ephorus.   For it is little short of
incredible that a writer of the rank of Ephorus should have
consented to adhere so closely both to the matter and the
style, either of his great rival Theopompus, or of the obscure
Cratippus.

Even those who deny the claims of Ephorus cannot but
admit that they find in the style of the fragment all the
characteristics that they would have expected to find in
Ephorus.   But the argument from style no longer rests on
what the ancient critics have told us of Ephorus.   The fragment already referred to, and another relating to the early
history of Sicyon,[2] which is most probably to be attributed to
Ephorus, enable us to judge, both of his style, and of the

[1] *Oxyrh. Pap.*, xiii, No. 1610.
[2] *Oxyrh. Pap.*, xi, No. 1365.   See inf. p. 144.

extent to which Diodorus incorporated his actual words in his own text. The style of these new fragments differs in no respect from the style of the Papyrus, while in those passages of Diodorus which are most likely to have preserved the language of his authority we find frequent coincidences with the Papyrus. In a writer whose style is tame we cannot expect to find rare or striking phrases. In such a case the relative frequency of certain of the ordinary words is perhaps as good a test as the occurrence of rare words in a writer of a different type. Some of the more characteristic phrases, however, in the fragment are found in Diodorus.

If the hypothesis which identifies the author of the fragment with Ephorus is accepted, we are in a far better position than we were before its discovery to judge of the merits of one of the most famous historians of antiquity. It was from Ephorus and Theopompus, rather than from Herodotus and Thucydides, that Cicero and the Roman writers generally derived their view of Greek history. The evidence which is now available, slight and fragmentary though it be, is at least sufficient to let us see that he cannot be ranked with Herodotus or Thucydides, either in respect of literary style or historical discernment. To borrow a famous phrase of the late Mr. Lecky's, ' the texture of his mind is commonplace'. There is no touch of distinction in his style, and his view of things too often rests upon the surface, instead of penetrating to their causes. He was the pupil of Isocrates, and he lived in an age dominated by rhetoric. Unfortunately for him, the spirit of rhetoric differs not a little from the spirit of truth. For all that, there can hardly be a doubt that in losing Ephorus we have lost much. He would have had a great deal to tell us of the earlier periods of Greek history which is not to be found in Herodotus, and some of it would have been of value. Of what he had to tell us of the period between the Persian and Peloponnesian Wars, and of the history of the fourth century, we can form some idea from the extant books of Diodorus, though it is certain that not a little that was omitted by Diodorus was of as much historical interest as that which he has preserved. It is for the period for which Xenophon is

our sole contemporary authority that we have most reason to
deplore the loss of Ephorus.   E. M. W.

For a fuller discussion of the subject see the Introduction
and Notes of Grenfell and Hunt in the *Oxyrhynchus Papyri*,
part v, No. 842; Eduard Meyer, *Theopomps Hellenika* (Berlin,
1909); E. M. Walker, *The Hellenica Oxyrhynchia; its Authorship and Authority* (Oxford, 1913).

The 'Athenian Constitution'.

There is much to be said for the view that of all the papyrological discoveries of the last thirty years that of Aristotle's
Athenian Constitution ranks first in importance. No one
would question the importance either of Aristotle or of the
constitutional history of Athens. It may be going too far to
assert that the chief interest of Greek history is to be found on
its constitutional side, but the history of that constitution
which was regarded by the Greeks themselves as the pattern
of democracy in the ancient world can hardly fail to appeal to
a generation in which, as in Aristotle's own time, democracy
seems likely to become the sole form of government. But the
importance of the discovery lies not merely in the author and
the subject. Of all the lost works of antiquity that have been
recovered this is one of the least fragmentary. Although the
beginning is lost and the last portion is mutilated, the part
that remains is at once much the greater portion of the treatise
and much the more important, while the lacunae in it are comparatively few.

The *Athenian Constitution* formed one of a series of constitutions, 158 in number, which treated of the institutions
of the various states in the Greek world, and which were
all attributed to Aristotle. The work, which is repeatedly
referred to by later writers, such as Plutarch, and by the
Scholiasts and Lexicographers, was extant until the seventh
century A. D., or to an even later date, but was subsequently
lost. Some very imperfect fragments of it (mere scraps, in
fact) were acquired by the Egyptian Museum at Berlin, and

were published in 1880. The great discovery came some ten
years later. Somewhere or other in Egypt, and somehow (the
secret has been well kept), a copy of this treatise, written in
four different hands upon four rolls of Papyrus, was acquired
by the Trustees of the British Museum, and was published by
them in 1891. The task of editing it was entrusted to Mr. (now
Sir) F. G. Kenyon, at that time an assistant in the Department
of Manuscripts.

Of one thing we may be certain, beyond any possibility of
doubt. The treatise acquired by the British Museum is
identical with the work that passed in antiquity under the
name of Aristotle. The evidence derived from a comparison
of the Papyrus with the quotations from Aristotle's *Athenian
Constitution* which are found in Plutarch, and in the Scholiasts
and Grammarians, is conclusive. Of fifty-eight quotations
from Aristotle's work, fifty-five occur in the Papyrus. Of
thirty-three quotations from Aristotle which relate to matters
connected with the constitution, or constitutional history, of
Athens, although they are not expressly referred to the
Constitution, twenty-three are found in the Papyrus. Of those
not found in the Papyrus, most appear to have come either from
the missing beginning or the mutilated end. The coincidence,
therefore, is as nearly as possible complete.

It follows that the only question as to authorship that
can be raised is the question whether the work is by
Aristotle, or by a pupil : i.e. as to the sense in which it is
Aristotelian.

When the Papyrus was first published, not a few voices were
raised against the attribution of the work to Aristotle himself.
The objections that were urged were based, partly on the contradictions between the *Constitution* and the *Politics*, and
partly on style. The contradictions are not many, but they
are important. They relate to the three most famous names
in the early history of the Athenian constitution—Draco,
Solon, and Cleisthenes. Chapter IV of the *Constitution* contains an account of a constitution which is ascribed to Draco ;
in the *Politics* it is expressly asserted that Draco left the constitution untouched. In the *Constitution* it is said that under

the Solonian constitution the archons were appointed by lot out of selected candidates, while in the *Politics* the election of the archons by the *Demos* is insisted on as being the chief safeguard provided by Solon for the liberty of the people. Finally the class enfranchised by Cleisthenes appears in the *Politics* as consisting of slaves and metics, while in the *Constitution* it is said to have been those free residents in Attica who were not of pure Athenian descent on both sides. The objections based on style are of two kinds: those that are based on the occurrence of non-Aristotelian words and phrases, and those that are based on the style, in the sense of the composition and general character of the work. Neither the objections based on the contradictions, nor those based on words and turns of expression, are in reality formidable. As the chapter relating to Draco is almost certainly an interpolation, the contradictions which are of moment are reduced to two. There is nothing in the least improbable in the suggestion that Aristotle, in the interval between the composition of the *Politics* and that of the *Constitution*, changed his mind both as to the appointment of the archons under the Solonian constitution and as to the class enfranchised by Cleisthenes. If in the former case he changed it for the worse, there can be no question that in the latter he changed it for the better. Those scholars who insisted on the differences between the vocabulary of the *Constitution* and that of the *Ethics* or *Politics* seem to have forgotten that such a difference is just what was to be expected when we are dealing in the one case with a historical work, intended for popular use, and in the other with philosophical treatises. As a matter of fact, an attentive study of the *Constitution* brings to light a surprising number of coincidences, both of thought and expression, between it and the *Politics*. The one strong argument against the attribution of the *Constitution* to Aristotle himself is that which is drawn from the general character of the work. It can hardly be denied that the work as a whole seems unworthy of the author of the undoubtedly genuine writings. If it is from the pen of Aristotle, then Aristotle as a historian stands on a lower level than we had imagined. There is no sense of proportion (we have only to contrast the space devoted to Peisistratus and his sons, or to the Revolutions of the Four Hundred and the Thirty, with the inadequate treatment of the period between the Persian and Peloponnesian Wars, to appreciate the force of this objection) ; there is an uncritical acceptance of erroneous views, and a general lack of historical insight ; and there is the undue prominence of the anecdotic element.

This objection by itself, however serious it may seem, cannot outweigh the arguments which have led to the general acceptance of the hypothesis that the author is Aristotle himself. In the first few years after the publication of the Papyrus there were a number of names that could be quoted on the other side. At the present moment it is doubtful if a single competent scholar can be found who would question Aristotle's authorship. The arguments in favour of attributing the work to Aristotle are as nearly conclusive as any such arguments ever can be. To begin with, there is the consensus of antiquity. Every ancient writer who mentions the *Constitution* ascribes it to Aristotle, and no critic in the ancient world is known to have called its genuineness in question. This consideration alone is all but sufficient. Secondly, the date which can with certainty, on grounds of internal evidence, be assigned to the *Constitution* coincides with the period of Aristotle's second residence in Athens. Finally, there are the parallelisms of thought and expression with passages in the *Politics* ; and these are of such a nature as to go a long way towards carrying conviction. It is easy to argue that a series such as the constitutions, no less than 158 in number, might naturally be entrusted to pupils working under the direction of their master. It is equally easy to reply that the *Athenian Constitution* would have been infinitely the most important of the series, and hence the one that would most properly be reserved for the master's hand. It may be added that there are no traces in the treatise either of variety of authorship or of incompleteness, though there is evidence of interpolation.

The work consists of two parts, the one narrative, and the other descriptive. The first forty-one chapters compose the former part, the rest of the treatise the latter.

The first part, when complete, contained an account of the original constitution of Athens and of the eleven changes through which it successively passed. The Papyrus, however, is imperfect at the beginning (the manuscript from which it was copied appears to have been similarly defective), the text commencing in the middle of a sentence which relates to the trial and banishment of the Alcmeonidae for the part that they had played in the suppression of Cylon's conspiracy. The missing chapters must have contained a sketch of the original constitution, and of the changes introduced in the time of Ion and Theseus. Chapters ii and iii give a description of the constitution before the time of Draco; chapter iv contains a summary account of a constitution which is ascribed to Draco; chapters v to xii are occupied with the reforms of Solon, both agrarian and constitutional. In chapter xiii we have an account of the party feuds that followed the reforms of Solon, and in chapters xiv to xix a much fuller narrative of the reign of Peisistratus and his sons. Chapters xx and xxi treat of the reforms of Cleisthenes, and chapter xxii of the changes introduced between Cleisthenes and the Invasion of Xerxes. The whole period between the Persian Wars and the Revolution of the Four Hundred (479–411 B.C.) is covered in six chapters (chapters xxiii–xxviii), while no less than twelve are allotted to the reactionary movements at the end of the fifth century (chapters xxix to xxxiii to the Four Hundred, and chapters xxxiv to xl to the Thirty). The narrative portion ends with chapter xli, which contains a list of the successive changes in the constitution.

The second part describes the constitution as it existed at the period of the composition of the treatise (329–322 B.C.). The subjects of which it treats are four. The conditions of citizenship and the training of the *ephebi* (citizens between the ages of 18 and 20); the Council ($\beta o \upsilon \lambda \acute{\eta}$); the magistrates; and the law-courts. The Ecclesia is dealt with only incidentally, in connexion with the *prytaneis* and *proedri*. The treatment of the first three subjects occupies chapters xlii to lxii. With chapter lxiii begins the section on the law-courts, but this portion, with the exception of chapter lxiii, is fragmentary in

character, owing to the mutilated condition of the fourth roll
of the papyrus on which it was written.

In the narrative part, while there is much of the utmost
value, there is much that cannot be accepted as true.   The
constitution of Draco in chapter iv is certainly unhistorical; it
is almost certainly an interpolation.   Equally unhistorical, in
the judgement of the present writer, are the restoration of the
ascendancy of the Areopagus after the Persian Wars, the
introduction of payment for the citizens by Aristides, the
association of Themistocles with Ephialtes in the overthrow
of the Areopagus, the part played by Damonides in inspiring
the policy of Pericles, and the course and implied chronology
of the Revolution of the Four Hundred.   What is hardly less
surprising than the acceptance of so much that is unhistorical
is the author's conception of his subject.   There is not a word
as to the constitution of the Empire in the fifth century.
That which constituted the greatness of Athens to Thucydides,
and which still gives to Athens the unique interest of its
history—the combination of democracy and empire—this
eludes him altogether.   The treatment, again, of that which is
in a sense the most important stage in the development of the
constitution, the period between Cleisthenes and the Peloponnesian War, is treated inadequately and with little insight.   We
would gladly have surrendered some of the anecdotes about
Peisistratus for a fuller account of the reforms of the Periclean
Age.   Strangest of all, we look in vain for any consistent view
of the Athenian democracy.   Such defects must not blind us
to the value of the work.   Thirty years ago we saw through
a glass darkly; now we see face to face.   Before the discovery
of the Papyrus our knowledge was fragmentary and all at
second hand.   Now at least we know what Aristotle really
said.   And much of what he has to tell us is at once true and
important.   There is the whole of the second part to begin
with.   As evidence of the practice of Aristotle's own time, it is
evidence that cannot be called in question.   It is dull reading
for the most part, it is true, and there must be something
wrong with a method which touches on the Ecclesia only
incidentally, but the last half of the *Constitution* must always

be our main authority for the institutions of the fourth century. And it is difficult for those who have begun their study of Greek history since 1891 to appreciate their debt to the historical narrative contained in the first part. For Solon we always had the excellent material contained in Plutarch's *Life*, but the new material afforded us in chapters ii to xiii of the *Constitution* throws a flood of light, not merely on the reforms themselves, but on the conditions, both economic and political, of pre-Solonian Athens, and on the period immediately following his legislation. For Cleisthenes we had no Plutarch to help us, and here the difference between our new knowledge and our former assumptions is as that between light and twilight. The chapters that are concerned with the period between Cleisthenes and the Four Hundred, however disappointing they may be in not a few respects, have conferred on us the inestimable boon of an accurate chronology of the constitutional development. Any number of questions round which controversy had raged are answered once and for all. The Areopagus certainly existed ages before Solon; it was Solon and not Cleisthenes who instituted the Heliaea ; in spite of Herodotus, the archons were not appointed by lot until after Marathon ; it was Ephialtes, not Pericles, who deprived the Areopagus of its powers. These are but a few examples of what we owe to the Papyrus. It is thanks too to the Papyrus that for the first time Ephialtes and Theramenes are seen in their true proportions. And it is thanks to it that we realize what we should never have guessed from Thucydides or Xenophon—the part played by the Moderates in the Revolutions of the Four Hundred and the Thirty.

The explanation of the defects to which we have called attention is twofold. It is to be found partly in the circumstances of the age in which the treatise was written, and partly in the method followed by Aristotle in its composition. There are two passages (xl. 1 and lxii. 2) which prove that the *Constitution* was written before the end of the Lamian War in the autumn of 322, when the democratic constitution was abolished and when Samos ceased to be one of the Athenian possessions. On the other hand, there are two passages (lxii. 2 and lxi. 1) which prove that it must be dated after the loss of all the foreign possessions of Athens, except Lemnos, Imbros, Scyros, Delos, and Samos, as the result of Chaeronea (338 B. C.), and after the institution of a special Strategus ἐπὶ τὰς συμμορίας, i. e. after 334 B. C. The dating of an event by the archonship of Cephisiphon (ch. liv. 7) enables us to fix still more precisely the years 329 and 322 as the limits of the period to which the composition of the work must be assigned. It follows that Aristotle wrote at the moment of the defeat and humiliation of Athens. To him, as to Demosthenes and his contemporaries, the Great Age of Athens was found not in the epoch of Pericles, but in that of the Persian Wars. The Empire had been her undoing. To understand the *Constitution* it is requisite to read it side by side with two of the most significant of the orations of Isocrates, the *de Pace* and the *Areopagiticus*. From the former of these is derived the view that the ναυτικὴ δύναμις had proved the ruin of Athens, in the light of the latter we may explain the prominence of the Areopagus in Aristotle's narrative. It is the method followed by the author in the composition of his work that explains the want of any consistent view of the constitution and the acceptance of so much that should have been rejected. It is comparatively easy to form a general estimate of Aristotle's indebtedness to previous writers, though difficult enough to determine in every case the precise source from which a passage is derived. Little comes from Thucydides and Xenophon. Herodotus was drawn upon more fully, both for the tyranny of Peisistratus and for the struggle between Cleisthenes and Isagoras. The poems of Solon are quoted at some length as evidence for the nature of his reforms. But the most important of his sources was unquestionably the *Atthis* of Androtion, a work published only a few years earlier than the *Constitution*. From it are derived, not only the passages which are annalistic in character and read like excerpts from a chronicle (e. g. ch. xiii. 1, 2 ; xxii ; xxvi. 2, 3), but also most of the matter common to the *Constitution* and Plutarch's *Solon*. The coincidences with Plutarch, which are often verbal, and extend to about 50 lines out of 170 in chs. v to xi of the

Constitution, are best explained on the hypothesis that Hermippus, the writer followed by Plutarch, used the same source as Aristotle, viz. the *Atthis* of Androtion. Another of his sources was a work written towards the end of the fifth century B. C., by a writer of oligarchical sympathies, with the object of defaming the character and policy of the heroes of the democracy. This source can be traced in passages such as vi. 2 (Solon's turning the Seisachtheia to the profit of himself and his friends), ix. 2 (the obscurity of Solon's laws intentional), and xxvii. 4 (Pericles' motive for the introduction of the dicasts' pay). Though the object and date of this pamphlet are fairly certain, its authorship is quite uncertain. One more source remains to be mentioned, second in importance only to the *Atthis* of Androtion: that from which are derived the accounts of the Four Hundred and the Thirty. The view taken of the character and course of the revolutions betrays a strong bias in favour of Theramenes, whose ideal is alleged to have been the πάτριος πολιτεία. A comparison of the *Constitution* with the relevant passages in Herodotus, or Plutarch's *Solon*, or with certain of the fragments of Androtion, reveals the fact that Aristotle followed his authorities with surprising fidelity. As these authorities were of very different value and of opposite sympathies, it is easy to explain why there is no consistency in the view taken of the Athenian constitution, and why so much that is untrue finds a place alongside of that which is historical.

Finally, it may be pointed out that there are two conclusions of first-rate importance which follow from the recovery of the *Constitution*. The first is the rehabilitation of the Scholiasts. All that they asserted to be contained in the *Constitution* is now found to be there. It is no longer admissible to brush aside with a light heart the testimony of a Scholiast when it happens to be inconvenient. There was a time when it could be argued that the Scholiast who states that Aristotle in the *Athenian Constitution* mentioned that Cleophon induced the Ecclesia to reject the terms of peace offered by the Spartans after Arginusae is clearly confusing Arginusae with Cyzicus, and that Aristotle in reality was referring to the

embassy described by Diodorus in connexion with the latter
battle. That time is past. The Scholiast was not mistaken.
It is Arginusae and not Cyzicus in Aristotle. No doubt, the
Scholiasts were sometimes stupid and misunderstood a passage
or a reference. What is certain is that they did not invent.

The second conclusion is one that affects the reputation of
Aristotle. There was a time when it could be assumed that
a statement must be true because it rested on the authority of
Aristotle, in the *Politics* or elsewhere. That time too is past.
When we come to examine the use that he makes of his
authorities we find that, though he occasionally compares,
criticizes, or combines, as a rule he adheres closely to the
writers whom he is consulting. His authority, even for the
history of the fifth century, is very far from being final. Nor
is there any evidence of independent inquiry, or of the utiliza-
tion of other sources than literary ones. And if an anecdote
suited his purpose, he did not stay to inquire into its authenticity. Between Aristotle, as a historian, and Thucydides
there is a great gulf fixed. The more that is recovered of the
ancient historians, and the more we learn of their methods, the
more there is brought home to us the unique greatness of
Thucydides in the field of historical criticism.   E. M. W.

Miscellaneous Historical Fragments.

A number of smaller fragments of historical works may be
mentioned together here. They illustrate the wide range of
Greek writers, and all have some interest.

1. It was known that Ptolemy I was an author, and wrote
an account of Alexander the Great's campaigns; indeed Grenfell and Hunt suggest him as the author of *Oxyrh. Pap.* iv,
No. 679. And now it is very probable that we have something
from the hand of his grandson,[1] Ptolemy Euergetes, in a fragment of parts of four columns dealing with the third Syrian
War, the so-called $Λαοδίκειος \ πόλεμος$ in 246 B.C. The

[1] Mahaffy, in *Petrie Papyri*, ii, No. xlv ; Mahaffy and Smyly, ib. iii,
p. 334 ; Holleaux, *Le Papyrus de Gourob*, in *Bull. Corr. Hell.* 30, 330.
Ptolemy VII, Physcon, in the next century, was an author also.

narrative is written in the first person, and the ἀδελφή mentioned would be Berenice. Ptolemy and Berenice, in command of an Egyptian fleet, are cruising along the coast of Syria. Berenice detaches a squadron to take treasure to Seleucia on the Orontes ; trouble arises there, but it is quelled, and when Ptolemy arrives he is received with enthusiasm. Then he proceeds to Antioch, where he receives an equally warm welcome. His style is more finished than that which his father Philadelphus uses in his dispatches, some of which have been preserved : the text of them is in *Archiv f. Papyrusforschung*, vi. 324 f. ; the two longest are from *Pap. Hal.*, i. 166, and *Inscr. v. Milet*, iii. n. 139, p. 300. The first is written in a royal and peremptory tone but negligent style, and was perhaps dictated from the king's own mouth ; the second is in a more formal tone, which is perhaps due to an official. Both are in the Κοινή. But it is perhaps unfair to judge Philadelphus by them.

2. Sosylus, possibly of Helos in Laconia,[1] is known to have written a history of Hannibal, with whom he had lived in camp. Polybius says contemptuously of him that his compositions are in the same class and have the same value as the chatter of the barber's shop and the quidnuncs (κουρεακῆς καὶ πανδήμου λαλιᾶς τάξιν ἔχειν καὶ δύναμιν).[2] Nothing however of the kind appears in this extract, which rather suggests a professional student of naval tactics.[3] Parts of four columns are preserved from the end of the fourth book, with the subscription :

Σωσύλου τῶν περὶ Ἀννίβου πράξεων δ.

It gives the account of the manœuvres of the fleets of the Massaliots and the Carthaginians in a sea-fight in which the Massaliots were successful. What the battle is cannot be determined for certain. Wilcken decides that in spite of difficulties it is the sea-fight off the mouth of the Ebro, described in Polyb. iii. 95. 5, and Livy xxii. 19. 5.

This is the first fragment from the original Greek sources for the history of the Punic Wars that has come to light.

[1] Susemihl, *Gr. Lit.* i. 636 n.   [2] Polyb. iii. 20.
[3] Published by U. Wilcken in *Hermes*, xli, p. 103.

3. An anonymous fragment of two columns from a history of Sicyon belongs to this period.[1] It deals with the origin and rise of Orthagoras, who was tyrant of Sicyon during part of the first half of the seventh century B. C., and an ancestor of Cleisthenes. Grenfell and Hunt think that the author may be Ephorus, or some one who derived his information from Ephorus.

4. Large fragments of Didymus's commentary on Demosthenes' *Philippics* contain extracts from Philochorus, the author of the Ἀτθίς.[2] They throw light on the campaign of Philip which ended with the battle of Chaeronea.

5. A fragment on the history of Sicily appears to be from an epitome, perhaps of the lost history of Sicily by Timaeus.[3]

A list of historical fragments will be found in Schubart's *Einführung in die Papyruskunde*, p. 477, s. v. 'Geschichte'.

J. U. P.

Satyrus's Life of Euripides.

' Biographi Graeci veteres mendacissimum genus hominum', is the terse comment of Dindorf when he discusses the authorities for the lives of the Greek dramatic poets. Yet we welcome an addition to our knowledge of Greek biography in this large fragment of a writer who continues the formal dialogue of Plato and Xenophon, and anticipates the narrative treatment of Plutarch.

It is little short of a commonplace that the ancient Greeks were singularly careless in the preservation of anything like an accurate record of the lives of great men. The principal reason of this is undoubtedly the scarcity of anything approaching literary record until the classical period was over. Until then it was the spoken, not the written, word which had the greater power.

The birth of criticism in its modern sense took place at Alexandria in the third century B. C., and there is no doubt

[1] *Oxyrh. Pap.* xi, No. 1365. Lenchantin De Gubernatis conjectures the author to be Menaechmus, the author of Σικυωνικά, a writer of the age of Alexander the Great (*Boll. di Fil. Class.* xxv. 129).

[2] *Berlin. Klass. Texte*, i; G. Glotz in *Bull. Corr. Hell.*, 1907, p. 526.

[3] *Oxyrh. Pap.* iv, No. 665.

that previous to this time anything like accurate biography was practically not thought of.

Yet the learned men of Alexandria did not turn to biography.

This department of literature became a monopoly of the Peripatetic School of Philosophers, who after the death of Strato in about 270 B.C., wholly abandoned philosophic research, and devoted themselves to the presentation of Ethics and History in a popular form. The best example of this method which has come down to us is given by the Characters of Theophrastus, their forerunner, who there presented the scientific analysis of human character in a popular and amusing way. These writers were journalists, popular, discursive, and uncritical, and scandalmongers who pandered to the low taste of their readers. The fragmentary references made by other writers to Peripatetic authors such as Aristoxenus, Heraclides Ponticus, Clearchus, Chamaeleon, Sotion, Hermippus, and in particular Hieronymus, appear to justify this verdict. The most striking feature in what little remains of their works is a passion for anecdote, and particularly for gossip of an unpleasant kind.

Hermippus indeed had learning; this is testified to by the use which Didymus made of him in his commentary on Demosthenes; but he, too, gratified the contemporary desire to listen to gossip. On the other hand, no modern writer on Characters has been as fresh and entertaining as Theophrastus, many of whose descriptions are anecdotes without names.[1]

Of Satyrus, the other notable Peripatetic biographer, more can be made out. He was a native of Callatis,[2] a town on the Black Sea, in the Dobrudscha. He probably lived in the third century B.C., and wrote lives of kings, statesmen, generals, orators, philosophers, and poets, which are often cited by Athenaeus and Diogenes Laertius. The Papyrus

[1] Aristoxenus wrote a περὶ Τραγῳδοποιῶν and Βίοι Ἀνδρῶν: Heraclides Ponticus, who at least fell under the Peripatetic influence, wrote on literary history, and probably touched on biography; Chamaeleon apparently wrote a Βίος Αἰσχύλου.
[2] Καλλατιανός, in a Βίος Σωκράτους from Herculaneum, probably by Philodemus; Crönert in *Rhein. Mus.* (1902), 57. 295.

formed part of this last section, that on poets, and was the sixth book in the collection. The more formal title, Βίων Άναγραφή, is found in the Papyrus. He also wrote Περὶ Χαρακτήρων, of which Athenaeus preserves a fragment, and probably he was the Satyrus who, according to Dionysius of Halicarnassus, collected ancient myths.

He also probably is to be identified with the author of a work on the Alexandrian Demes. The fragments of his writings have been collected by Müller in the third volume of his *Fragmenta Historicorum Graecorum*, together with a moderately amusing passage about Diogenes the Cynic preserved by St. Jerome, in the fourth. His lives were summarized by Heraclides Lembus in the second century, and Dr. Hunt notes it as a curious coincidence that Heraclides, whom Suidas calls 'Οξυρυγχίτης, probably lived 'in the city from the ruins of which the present Papyrus was obtained'. Diogenes Laertius calls him a native of Callatis, like Satyrus.[1]

The Life of Euripides by Satyrus, discovered in 1911, and published by Dr. Hunt in *Oxyrhynchus Papyri*, ix, No. 1176, contains a number of lamentable lacunae, but enough is preserved to show its character. Contrary to what we should have expected, the work is cast in the form of a dialogue, which seems an extraordinary method to apply to biography ; but in this connexion it is noteworthy that Aristotle also used the dialogue in his work Περὶ Ποιητῶν, and Clearchus in his books Περὶ Βίων. It is more surprising to find that at least one of the interlocutors is a woman : her name is given as Εὔκλεια. Another character is addressed more than once in the vocative case, but on each occasion the manuscript gives us ω Διοδωρ[, breaking off at the final letter : Dr. Hunt adds the masculine, von Arnim the feminine termination. The introduction of a second female character is thus a possibility ; and the fact that this person champions the cause of women makes it a probability. The third character is presumably a man, and his attitude, as shown in such words as πλὴν ταῦτα μὲν συνηγορήσθω ταῖς γυναιξίν· ἐπανάγωμεν δὲ πάλιν ἐπὶ τὸν Εὐριπίδην, seems to confirm the inference. This person (whom

[1] v. 94 Καλλατιανὸς ἢ 'Αλεξανδρεύς.

Leo rather improbably thinks may be Satyrus himself) stands to the others somewhat in the relation of a tutor to his pupils : at any rate he answers the questions and confirms the suggestions of the others, while in at least one case he recalls the others when wandering too far from the subject in hand. The method of dialogue is clearly used in order to present the subject-matter in a more attractive form and to provide a link between a number of unconnected anecdotes.

The style of the fragment is correct and polished, the dialogue is graceful, and its transitions skilful ; the choice of words is directed by good taste, and, as Dr. Hunt has pointed out in his preface to the fragment, there has been a fairly consistent effort to avoid hiatus. There is a punning and complimentary allusion to the name Εὔκλεια, and a quotation from Euripides, in which the same word occurs, appears to have been introduced in order to create the same effect. The general impression is that the dialogue takes place in a house (in Eucleia's *salon*, Schubart believes) between persons of good breeding, who take pleasure in polite conversation.

The author appears to have discussed Euripides at considerable length, and under various aspects. The fragments connected with his place in tragedy are not many, but the judgement that ηὖξεν καὶ ἐτελείωσεν ὥστε τοῖς μετ' αὐτὸν ὑπερβολὴν μὴ λιπεῖν conveys a sound piece of literary criticism. The influence of Anaxagoras and Socrates on him is discussed, but in the text as preserved there is no trace of the unkind story told by Suidas, that Euripides gave up philosophy because of the danger in which Anaxagoras was involved on account of his views. Then comes the influence of Euripides on subsequent literature : τὰ κατὰ τὰς περιπετείας, βιασμοὺς παρθένων, ὑποβολὰς παιδίων, ἀναγνωρισμοὺς διά τε δακτυλίων καὶ διὰ δεραίων· ταῦτα γάρ ἐστι δήπου τὰ συνέχοντα ('chief elements', H. P. Richards) τὴν νεωτέραν κωμῳδίαν, ἃ πρὸς ἄκρον ἤγαγεν Εὐριπίδης : this idea of Euripides as the literary ancestor of the authors of the New Comedy is suggestive and betrays critical insight, and the story that Philemon had a great admiration for him is met with in the *Βίος καὶ Γένος Εὐριπίδου* printed in Dindorf's *Poetae Scaenici*. The religious and political views of Euripides are discussed. There are a number of new quotations, while those previously known in some places confirm conjectures made by earlier scholars. Anecdotes are plentiful. Satyrus is our earliest authority for the famous story that Athenian prisoners of war in Sicily found favour with their captors through knowledge of Euripides; and in addition to our former knowledge, that the poet encouraged Timotheus when his works met with a cold reception, we learn a new piece of information, that he wrote the prelude of the Πέρσαι for him : this is interesting, since large fragments of this work were published by Wilamowitz in 1903 shortly after their discovery.[1]

The scholars who have written on Satyrus are shy about accepting this statement.[2] The account is circumstantial, and is as follows:

Fr. 39, col. xxii : ⟨ἀδοξοῦντος δέ, or καταφρονουμένου ?⟩ τοῦ Τιμοθέου παρὰ τοῖς Ἕλλησιν διὰ τὴν ἐν τῇ μουσικῇ καινοτομίαν καὶ καθ' ὑπερβολὴν ἀθυμήσαντος ὥστε καὶ τὰς χεῖρας ἑαυτῷ διεγνωκέναι προσφέρειν, μόνος Εὐριπίδης ἀνάπαλιν τῶν μὲν θεατῶν καταγελάσαι, τὸν δὲ Τιμόθεον αἰσθόμενος ἡλίκος ἐστὶν ἐν τῷ γένει παραμυθήσασθαί τε λόγους διεξιὼν ὡς οἷόν τε παρακλητικωτάτους, καὶ δὴ καὶ τὸ τῶν Περσῶν προοίμιον συγγράψαι, τῷ τε νικῆσαι παύσασθαι καταφρονούμενον [αὐτίκα] τὸν Τιμόθεον.

'When Timotheus was unpopular (?) with the Greeks owing to his innovations in music, and became so exceedingly depressed that he had decided to make away with himself, Euripides alone took a contrary view, and poured ridicule upon the audience; and, perceiving the high quality of Timotheus's art, consoled him in the most encouraging terms possible, and also composed the opening of the Persae. So Timotheus by his success [soon] ceased to be despised.'

This anecdote appears in Plutarch in the following form [An seni sit ger. R. P. p. 795 D] Τιμόθεον Εὐριπίδης συριττόμενον ἐπὶ τῇ καινοτομίᾳ καὶ παρανομεῖν εἰς τὴν μουσικὴν δοκοῦντα θαρρεῖν ἐκέλευσεν ὡς ὀλίγου χρόνου τῶν θεάτρων ὑπ' αὐτῷ γενησομένων.

---

[1] See pp. 59 sqq. above.

[2] The single line from the opening of the Persae which Plutarch preserves (Bergk, P. L. G. iv, Tim. Fr. 8), and the extremely mutilated opening in the Papyrus of Timotheus, throw no light on the question.

Euripides liked innovations and knew his public. What is
more likely than that he should have wished to make his
prophecy come true, and have lent the unpopular author a
helping hand? There is a little historical difficulty in connexion with the performance of the *Persae* and Euripides'
death; but the story cannot be disproved.

The dates are fairly certain; the death of Euripides in
406 B.C., and the performance of the *Persae* in about 400 B.C.
(as Wilamowitz now thinks). At first sight they appear to
conflict. But it is a common fallacy to suppose that, because
a play was produced or a poem first published in a given
year, the play or the poem was actually composed in that
year. We need only assume that the poem was composed
some time before it was performed, and then Euripides may
have had a hand in it.[1]

The debt of Euripides to Anaxagoras has often been discussed, and Satyrus says that it was considerable: τὸν [Ἀνα]ξα-
γόραν [δαιμ]ονίως [ζηλώσας Leo] . . . ., Fr. 37, col. i (followed
by three quotations, the second of which is lost in a lacuna; the
first and the third were already known to us in a longer form),
and then ἀκριβῶς ὅλως περιείληφεν τὸν Ἀναξαγόρειον [διά]κο-
σμον [ἐν] τρισὶ περι[όδοις, 'he has with precision and complete-
ness summed up Anaxagoras's cosmic system in three periods'.
This adds some information, but needs to be explained. The
first quotation is from the *Peirithous* (573 Nauck); the second
was contained in a lacuna between the end of the second
column and the beginning of the third; the third quotation we
have already in a longer form (Frag. Inc. 912), attributed by

---

[1] The statement has been made that Euripides 'lived in a cave' in
Salamis, implying that he was an unsociable eccentric who became a
troglodyte. Aulus Gellius's absurd adjectives (xv. 20) seem to imply the
same thing: 'Philochorus refert in insula Salaminia speluncam esse
taetram et horridam, quam nos vidimus, in qua Euripides tragoedias
scriptitarit.' This rests on a misconception. Satyrus's words, [κεκτη]μένος
σπήλαιον τὴν ἀναπνοὴν ἔχον εἰς τὴν θάλατταν, ἐν τούτῳ διημέρευεν καθ' αὑτὸν
μεριμνῶν ἀεί τι καὶ γράφων (Fr. 39, col. ix), and the words in the Βίος (Schwartz,
Eurip. Schol. Γένος, s. 5), σπήλαιον κατασκευάσαντα ἀναπνοὴν ἔχον εἰς τὴν
θάλασσαν ἐκεῖσε διημερεύειν φεύγοντα τὸν ὄχλον, simply mean that he 'fitted
up' a cave as a study by the seaside, like a summer bungalow. This was
probably the place ἐν ᾧ σχολάζων ἐτύγχανεν where the women were said to
have set upon him (Sat., col. x; comp. Γένος, s. 5).

Valckenaer and von Arnim to the *Cretans*. But we are now able to see, as Leo[1] points out, that this is also from the *Peirithous*, and that each quotation formed a περίοδος, a ' periodic ' sentence, the three ' periods ' comprising the whole Anaxagorean system. Other new pieces of information are, that Euripides' retirement from Athens was partly due to his irritation with the poets Acestor, Dorilaus, Morsimus, and Melanthius ; and that Cleon prosecuted him for impiety ; which is not so incredible as it seems at first sight, considering the levity with which such charges were made.

Mr. W. R. Paton[2] has pointed out two reminiscences of Satyrus in the writings of Plutarch, but his influence is most clearly seen in the Βίος καὶ Γένος of Euripides, many passages in which are verbally identical with passages in Satyrus's biography ; the parallels have been admirably collected by Körte ; but it is obvious from even a cursory comparison that Satyrus had as much influence as any other author on the formation of the Βίος καὶ Γένος. It might therefore be reasonably expected that his biographies would have had similar influence on the traditional lives of Aeschylus and Sophocles ; and an examination of these seems to justify the expectation ; probably the other ' Lives ' of Satyrus were of much the same type and, in the case of the tragedians, took the form of a dialogue between the same three characters as in the Life of Euripides. Satyrus is actually referred to in the Life of Sophocles, and the three current Βίοι are certainly formed on much the same lines ; there is the same scarcity of definite fact, the same abundance of anecdotes, while a large number of the anecdotes are concerned with literary criticism. There are however one or two features which seem more emphatically to betray a common origin. Aeschylus is said to have left Athens for the court of Hiero, because the Athenians failed to appreciate him sufficiently, and Sophocles was so exceedingly patriotic that he resisted the tempting invitations of many βασιλεῖς : these incidents are certainly paralleled by the story told by Satyrus that Euripides was

---

[1] *Götting. gel. Anz.*, 1912, pp. 273 sqq.
[2] *Class. Rev.* xxvii, p. 131.

driven to Macedonia by the preference accorded to minor
poets (Fr. 39, col. xv): in fact the tradition followed by Satyrus
appears to have been distinctly hostile to Athens, as is indicated by the passage, τὰ μὲν γὰρ τῶν Ἀθήνησιν οὐδὲ λέγειν
ἄξιον, οἵ γε ποιητὴν τηλικοῦτον Μακεδόνων καὶ Σικελιωτῶν
ὕστερον ᾔσθοντο (Fr. 39, col. xix). Another passage in the Life
of Aeschylus—αἵ τε διαθέσεις τῶν δραμάτων οὐ πολλὰς περιπετείας καὶ πλοκὰς ἔχουσιν ὡς παρὰ τοῖς νεωτέροις—is echoed by
the passage (already quoted) in the new fragments, where the
περιπέτειαι and (though the word is not used) πλοκαί of Euripides are regarded as the precursors of the New Comedy ;
and the expression in the Life of Sophocles, Σοφοκλέους μέλιτι
τὸ στόμα κεχριμένον, suggests a passage in Satyrus's Life
(col. xx), ἔχει τὸ στόμα καὶ [καθ' ὑπ]ερβολὴ[ν δυσῶδες], to
which the reply is made : ' What mouth has been such, or
could be sweeter than that from which proceed odes and
dialogue (μέλη τε καὶ ἔπη) like his ? '

It is unfortunate for Satyrus's reputation that he chose to
cast his biographies in dialogue form, and still more unfortunate
that the Oxyrhynchus Life has reached us in so mutilated
a condition. These facts excuse or explain the adverse
criticisms which have been passed on his work by distinguished
scholars. Thus Professor Murray writes, ' Evidently anecdotes
amused Satyrus and facts, as such, did not. He cared about
literary style, but he neither knew nor cared about history.' [1]
Against this judgement it might suffice to quote the more
kindly comment of Professor Hunt, ' A fondness for anecdote,
which Satyrus shares with his kind, and which was a product
of the prevailing interest in individual character and personal
traits and details, does not necessarily imply an uncritical turn
of mind. The tales are commonly prefaced with the warning
" as they relate ", " as is said ", and the like.' In addition to
this even in its present condition the text allows us to see that
the traditional stories are very largely only introduced by one
interlocutor to be refuted or at least criticized by the succeeding speaker. Thus the story of the Thesmophoriazusae (Fr. 39,

---

[1] *Euripides and His Age*, p. 24.

col. x) is followed by the quotation of a passage in praise of
women taken from Euripides' *Melanippe*; the scandal about
Cephisophon (Fr. 39, col. xii–xiii) by some pertinent remarks
on the folly of judging all women by the conduct of one ; the
disparagement of Euripides in Fr. 39, col. xvi (for such appears
to be the point of the quotation), by the remark ἐοίκασιν
ἀνδρὸς εἶναι τῶν ἀντιδιδασκόντων αὐτῷ, καθάπερ εἶπες· ἀτὰρ
σιναμώρως γε κἀνταῦθα πάλιν ὁ κωμῳδοδιδάσκαλος ἐπέδακνεν
τὸν Εὐριπίδην ('mischievous backbiting'), which shows that
Satyrus was conscious of the insecurity of the evidence.

Even the story of Euripides' death, which is referred to
Macedonian sources,[1] may very possibly have been criticized
in the lacuna following col. xxi.

In connexion with this it is interesting to note that, if
von Arnim is right in reading the feminine form Διοδώρα,
Satyrus had the original idea of choosing his defender of
Euripides from the very sex which he was commonly supposed
to have maligned bitterly.

In view of the nature of his material it was impossible for
Satyrus to reach modern standards of biographical accuracy,
and the method of *pro* and *con.* which he has adopted may,
unless carefully watched, give a misleading impression ; still he
does seem to have exercised a commonsense judgement on
the more extravagant details of the traditional story.

L. C. St. A. L.

---

[1] ὡς οἱ λόγιοί τε καὶ γεραίτατοι μυθολογοῦσι Μακεδόνων.

VII

ORATORY

LYSIAS AND HYPERIDES

Lysias.

THE longest of the new fragments of Lysias were discovered at Oxyrhynchus in 1905, and are published in vol. xiii of the series. The first fragments are the relics of a speech against a certain Hippotherses, the circumstances of which are peculiar.

Lysias had already been known as an opponent of the Thirty. They had killed his brother Polemarchus, for whose murder Lysias prosecuted Eratosthenes. The fragments lately discovered reveal another grievance. He had been robbed of his property as well,[1] but it is exceedingly difficult to reconstruct the orator's argument from the scanty remains that have been preserved. The speech is described as 'against Hippotherses in defence of a maid-servant':[2] how the maid-servant was concerned in the case is somewhat of a mystery. It appears that Lysias fled to the Peiraeus when his brother was murdered and that the Thirty seized his property. On his return he was unable to recover it even by paying the price to the purchasers.[3] The amnesty had provided that all who had bought property during the reign of terror should retain it, but that exiles should recover only what was unsold;[4] land and houses, however, were to be returned to their original owners.

It is clear enough that the case depended upon the exact interpretation of the words of the agreement. Hippotherses and his partners ought to have found little difficulty in inventing some plausible defence, relying on the strict letter of the law, while Lysias would be compelled to rely upon the only arguments which would be likely to prevail at a time when

---

[1] Fr. 6 ἀνόμως χρημάτων ἀπεστερημένος.
[2] Ib. fin. ὑπὲρ θεραπαίνης.   [3] Fr. 1.   [4] Fr. 4.

party passions were still running high ; these arguments, the equity of the case,[1] and Lysias's own patriotic actions[2] are touched upon with the simplicity and strength which the orator cultivated. He recounts his services to Athens at some length ; though he was a resident alien, he equipped a body of three hundred mercenaries and was active both in supplying and raising money. His opponent he describes as an enemy of Athens and its democracy, as his flight to Decelea proved.[3] The conclusion is remarkably brief and dignified, consisting of a bare half-dozen lines, devoid of all rhetorical excess and admirable in directness.

The next speech was delivered against Theomnestus by a person who had formerly been his friend. He had lent the defendant thirty minae, when he had to pay that sum to a certain Theozotides or become liable for an action. The money was lent without any witnesses being present ; as the borrower denied the loan the action was brought against him. The argument becomes obscure, but the plaintiff produces evidence that Theomnestus must have been at some time possessed of considerable money, as he provided a chorus for the festival of Dionysus.[4]

The remaining fragments are too scanty for any discussion of their contents. In the connected pieces there are to be found everywhere the marks of the genuine Lysias. The tone is subdued ; 'purple patches' are studiously avoided ; in fact, we are here face to face with the true classical spirit which cares little for individual strokes but everything for the general effect. It is enough to say that the total impression which these fragments produce is precisely the same as that caused by the speeches previously known ; that is, they bear witness to the excellence of the best Attic style.

Fragments of a speech against Theozotides were discovered in 1906 at Hibeh. The subject of the speech seems to have been a proposal by the defendant to cut down the pay of the Athenian cavalry from a drachma to four obols, but to raise the pay of the mounted archers from two obols to eight per day ;

---

[1] Fr. 5.   [2] Fr. 6.   [3] Ib.   [4] Ib.

the consequence was the 'stringing up' of the mercenary system,[1] a step which the orator rightly viewed with regret. Along with this proposal, or perhaps in consequence of it, Theozotides seems to have been anxious to refuse to maintain the adopted or illegitimate children of the Athenian soldiers, limiting the privilege of sustenance to those born in wedlock. Lysias points out the evil consequences which would happen if at the Dionysiac festival the herald, who read out the decree for the maintenance of fatherless children, were to limit the generosity of the State to one class only. The speech evidently would be one capable of arousing the greatest interest. It was the decline in the numbers of Athenian troops and the ever-increasing numbers of the mercenaries which eventually led to the Macedonian conquest so long opposed by the next orator, whose recently-discovered remains now call for discussion.

Hyperides.[2]

Before 1890 the published work of Hyperides consisted of the speeches in defence of Lycophron and Euxenippus, against Demosthenes and the Epitaphius, which were found in the middle of the last century in Egypt. In 1888 the speech against Athenogenes was also discovered there. The manuscript is in the Louvre, and is of the second century B. C. In 1890 the speech against Philippides was discovered in a manuscript of the same period, which contains also the third letter of Demosthenes. In 1905 another speech for Lycophron was found at Oxyrhynchus, and was published in 1919 in vol. xiii of the Oxyrhynchus Series. Hyperides accordingly as a literary find is entirely the child of Egypt.

The fragment of the speech against Philippides contains the concluding portion. Philippides had proposed a vote of thanks to one of the bodies of πρόεδροι for their having carried in the Ecclesia a motion in compliment to Philip of Macedon.

---

[1] συντείνειν τὴν μισθοφορίαν.

[2] See Hyperides, *The Orations against Athenogenes and Philippides*, F. G. Kenyon, London, Bell, 1893; and *Hyperidis Orationes et Fragmenta*, F. G. Kenyon, Clarendon Press, 1906.

There was some technical objection to the motion, but the πρόεδροι, acting under compulsion, persisted in their point. Hyperides admits that the necessity was one which could not have been avoided ; his contention is not against their action, but against Philippides for having proposed a vote of thanks to a body which had violated the constitution. The occasion therefore was important; it gave the orator, a strong nationalist, a chance of testing the attitude of public opinion towards the Macedonian party, of which Philippides was a member. He used the opportunity to bring the machinery of the γραφὴ παρανόμων to bear against his political enemy. After the passing of the vote of thanks to Philip and before the arraignment of Philippides, the King of Macedon seems to have died. The speech accordingly was delivered probably in the later portion of 336 B. C. or early in the next year.

One or two vivid touches bring the Macedonian party clearly before our eyes. Their record was bad. Their one principle was not love of any foreign power, but hatred of Athens. In support of Philippides was to be found Democrates, who seems to have been a descendant of Harmodius or Aristogiton. On the strength of his birth he enjoyed the privilege of maintenance at the public expense, which he used to deliver unpatriotic speeches in the Ecclesia. Philippides himself seems to have been far from respectable. He had already been twice convicted of illegal proposals ; Hyperides then had a strong case against a wilful offender which he pleads with force and skill. His legal contention is unanswerable; there can be no defence for a gratuitous proposal to compliment a body of committee-men who had acted illegally. The personal arguments are as good as these can ever be. Philippides' desire to curry favour with a despot is shown to be his main motive ; it defeated itself through the tyrant's death, while any claim to the pity of the court had been made impossible by the joy the defendant showed at every Athenian defeat. In short, the man at the bar is an unscrupulous political tool, whose speedy punishment is demanded by justice and expediency alike.

The speech against Athenogenes takes us out of the region

of politics. It is a lucky find, as it enables us to appreciate the grounds of criticism of the author of the famous treatise on Sublimity, who expressly mentions[1] this very speech in his favourable verdict on Hyperides. A young man, whose name is not preserved, wished to secure the person of a young boy who was the property of one Athenogenes, an Egyptian alien, who carried on three perfumery businesses in Athens. The youth, on approaching the owner of the slave, was informed that he could not have the boy without taking also his father Midas, and his brother, who were engaged in the business. In order to lure the youth into the purchase, Athenogenes employed a loose woman of some personal charms, Antigona by name, to cry up the value of the three slaves. The youth, being a mere gentleman-farmer, was no match for the woman and the business man, who was a professional attorney as well. Athenogenes recommended him not to buy their freedom from him, but to buy them outright: in this case he could do as he liked with them, without interference. There were a few paltry debts contracted by Midas in carrying on the perfumery business, but these would easily be liquidated by the sale of the stock in the shop itself. The plaintiff managed to scrape together the purchase-money from his own assets, assisted by the generosity of his friends. When he went to Athenogenes with the money, the latter produced a document already drawn up, which he read aloud and sealed in the presence of witnesses on the spot, to prevent a discussion of its contents by any inconvenient outsiders. No sooner had the sale been completed, than creditors sprang up demanding the payment of debts which Midas had incurred, and which were legally recoverable from his master. The total amount of these debts was five talents, a sum which it was beyond the plaintiff's power to pay ; and a personal interview with Athenogenes proving ineffectual, he was compelled to bring the present action against him.

Hyperides arranges his defence under two main heads. First, he urges the legal aspect of the case. The contract was concluded by fraud ; in the selling of slaves the law demanded

[1] Ch. xxxiv.

a mention of all infirmities in them. False pretences invalidated the betrothal of free persons and any testamentary dispositions they might make. Equity pointed to the corresponding illegality of the sale effected by Athenogenes.

In the next place he argues the case from the business point of view. Athenogenes had pretended that he did not know what the amount of the debts was. The plaintiff answered that he, though not a business man, had discovered them in less than three months. Any liabilities incurred by a slave should be discharged by the master who originally received the sums, not the master who purchased them later on. Solon's law expressly confirmed this contention, inasmuch as it required payment from the master who employed them.

He concludes by attacking the defendant's political actions. In order to evade military service at the time of the battle of Chaeronea, he moved to Troezen, where he married his daughters. Through the patronage of Mnaseas of Argos (a pro-Macedonian traitor), he was appointed archon in Troezen, but used his authority to banish the Troezenians, who fled to Athens for shelter, where they were at that very day, ready to bear witness to the truth of the accusations. On these three grounds the plaintiff called for the summary condemnation of a traitor and tyrant.

The next fragment [1] has not been ascribed by scholars to Hyperides without hesitation. It is a speech in defence of the Lycophron for whom the orator composed another which is still extant. [2] Lycophron had been accused of adultery with a woman whose husband was dying. The same names occur in both these orations, delivered about 340 B. C. The probability is that Hyperides composed two speeches for the defendant. The first, delivered by Lycophron himself, is the speech *For Lycophron*; the other, i. e. the Oxyrhynchus fragment, was delivered either by one of Lycophron's friends or possibly by the orator himself. On the whole the balance of opinion seems to be in favour of treating the latter as a genuine piece of Hyperides' work, although tradition is silent about any second speech for Lycophron which could be

[1] *Oxyrh. Pap.* 1607   [2] Hyper. *Lycophr.* (Kenyon, i).

identified with this fragment, which is only of inconsiderable extent.

The value of this recently recovered material is appreciable. First, it reveals to us more clearly the figure of a genuinely patriotic Athenian who supported Demosthenes against Macedon. The political arguments, so strange to us, are such as we would have expected from the traditional account of the man. We should remember the intensity of political life in a small city in which it was impossible for any citizen to escape public notice whether he were a traitor or a patriot.[1] The Macedonian influence at Athens was deeply resented: Hyperides himself twice protested against the action of Olympias in trumping up a cause for complaint in the matter of an Athenian dedication to Dione at Dodona, the primaeval seat of Greek worship;[2] he assures us that the very children in the schools knew all about the hirelings who extolled Macedonia and welcomed Philip's ambassadors in their houses or greeted them publicly in the streets.[3] Strictly speaking, the real ground for condemnation or acquittal of a defendant is the tendency his actions create towards the destruction or survival of a state as a whole. To the modern mind, the great power which maintains national existence is nothing more or less than morality ; 'Righteousness exalteth a nation'. But to a Greek the great power behind his country was patriotism ; if the defendant has displayed genuine patriotism, the orators rarely scruple to parade the fact as an argument, relying on the same appeal to that which preserved their state as is made by the modern pleader. The substance of the two arguments is the same, but the form which they take is entirely different. Both are irrelevant if applied to an age which was unsuited to them; each is appropriate in its own peculiar setting of time and circumstances.

But it is in the recently recovered speech against Athenogenes that the real Hyperides stands most clearly revealed. The other speeches are instances of pleading on subjects treated by

---

[1] Ib. § 14 λαθεῖν γὰρ τὸ πλῆθος τὸ ὑμέτερον οὐκ ἔνι οὔτε πονηρὸν ὄντα οὐδένα τῶν ἐν τῇ πόλει οὔτε ἐπιεικῆ.

[2] *Euxenipp.* 24.   [3] Ib. 22.

other orators ; in this speech we have an instance of a theme in which he admittedly was supreme. Longinus [1] singled out his handling of this very lawsuit (together with the action against Phryne) for his special commendation. The subject was one which required the dexterous handling of an accomplished 'man about town '. Throughout the speech the qualities of such a character stand out with great clearness.

In the first place there was no express law which rendered Athenogenes liable : the argument rests entirely upon considerations of equitable dealing. The case would be a disastrous failure if it were treated by an advocate whose touch was not light as well as sure ; commendation and suggestion are here in place, but not thunderous declamation or high-flown rhetoric. The tone of the speech is firm but rather subdued ; the language is easy and at times racy, if not colloquial with a slight touch of slang.[2] Again, the characters are such as would rouse the greatest social interest. The plaintiff was a young country gentleman,[3] quite ignorant of the tricks of business men, carried away by an impulsive attraction for a handsome slave ; the defendant was a professional speech-writer and an Egyptian,[4] working hand in glove with a clever procuress,[5] for whom the intended victim was an easy prey.[6] The feelings of the jury to which the appeal is made are precisely the same as those which are addressed in the political speeches, nationality and patriotism ; it was the property of an Athenian who had a stake in his country which was to be saved from ruin at the hands of an Egyptian who deserted Athens when she most needed him.

The rhetorical devices employed are similarly subdued, but subtle. Longinus, contrasting Hyperides with Demosthenes, says that the latter, when he tried to be amusing and witty, made himself a laughing-stock ; that his efforts to secure grace

---

[1] de Subl. ch. 34.

[2] προσπεριέκοψεν (§ 2) 'pocketed'; παιδαγωγηθῆναι (§ 3) 'gulled'; ἃ ἦν βραχέα τε καὶ ἐξῆν αὐτοῖς εἰπεῖν (§ 10) is colloquial ; κατατεμνόντων αὐτόν (§ 12) 'having a cut at'; εἰς τὴν ὠνὴν ἐνεσείσθην (§ 26) 'jockeyed into'; colloquialisms had already been noted in this author.

[3] § 26.

[4] § 3 λογογράφον τε καὶ ἀγοραῖον, τὸ δὲ μέγιστον, Αἰγύπτιον.

[5] δεινοτάτη ibid.   [6] § 2 ἐξίστησιν ἡμῶν τὴν φύσιν ἔρως.

defeated themselves; if he had attempted the little speech against Athenogenes he would have commended Hyperides even more.[1] The speech justifies this criticism. There are no long flowing periods, no complicated contrasts, no elaborate intricacies. Everything is smooth, easy, delightful. Yet the artist is there too. Traces of his craft appear in antithesis,[2] short periods, and careful technical finish.[3] In short the whole speech is that of a man perfectly at his ease, sure of triumph through the very grace of his art.

These qualities make Hyperides an ideal author for those who are anxious to acquire the easy tone of urbanity which is characteristic of a complex civilization. The 'plain style' of Lysias offers hardly the same attractions, much less the thunderous vigour of Demosthenes. Hence it is not strange to find that Hyperides was well known in Egypt. The same features which made Menander popular in that highly civilized land with its long traditions of ordered society, were present in Hyperides also. The transparent clearness of their language, the perfectly concealed art, the tone of self-confidence, and, above all, the knowledge of the world which both displayed, made them well worthy to be considered the best types of the period of Athenian culture which most closely resembled that of Egypt.

T. W. L.

---

[1] Ch. 34 τό γέ τοι περὶ Φρύνης ἢ ᾿Αθηνογένους λογίδιον ἐπιχειρήσας γράφειν ἔτι μᾶλλον ἂν ῾Υπερίδην συνέστησεν.

[2] οὐκ ἀπολόγημα ἀλλ᾿ ὁμολόγημα § 20.

[3] § 20, two instances; § 32, a good example.

INDEX

INDEX

164 INDEX

Demetrius Lacon, 40.
Demosthenes, 144, 160, 161; Hyperides' speech against, 155.
Diatribe, 1.
Didymus, 144.
Diodorus Siculus, 124, 128 sqq.
Diogenes Babylonius, 25.
    ,, the Cynic, 5.
    ,, Laertius, sources of, 26.
    ,, of Oenoanda, 31 sqq.
Diomede, Epyllion on, 109.
Diphilus, 79.
Dithyramb, 41, 61.
Dium, Paean from, 47.
Dorilaus, 150.

Egyptian society, 161.
Ἔλεγχος, 79 n.
Ephorus, 124, 128 sqq., 144.
Epicharmea, pseud-, 18 sqq.
Epicharmus, 11, 19, 114.
Epicureanism, 22.
Epicurus, 31 sqq., 40; Sententiae, 34.
Epidaurus, 46, 50.
Epigrams of Callimachus, the, 99.
Ἐπιτάφιος λόγος of Hyperides, the, 155.
Ἐπιτρέποντες of Menander, the, 68, 69, 91 sqq.
Epyllion, 109 sqq.
Erythrae, Paean from, 47.
Ἠθικὴ Στοιχείωσις of Hierocles, the, 36.
Eunuchus of Terence, the, 87.
Εὐφωρατίς (Scolion), 58.
Euphorion, 110, 111.
Euripides, 8, 80, 95, 121, 147 sqq.; Satyrus's Life of, 144 sqq.
Eurytheus, 50.
Eustathius, 109.
Euxenippus, Hyperides' speech for, 155.

Farce, 121.
Fortune, Lyric on, 59.

Gauls, invasion of the, 44, 45, 106, 107.
Γεωργός of Menander, the, 85, 91, 96.
Γνῶμαι, 18; of Epicurus, 34.
Golden Age, Poem on the, 107.
Grenfellianum Fragmentum, 54.

Hannibal, 143.
Hecale of Callimachus, the, 99, 103.

Helen, Lament of, Anon. Lyric, 55.
Ἡνίοχος of Menander, the, 90.
Heracles and Theiodamas (Callimachus), 102.
Heraclides Lembus, 146.
    ,, Ponticus, 145 n.
Herculaneum, Papyri of, 21, 27 sqq., 40.
Hermarchus, 21, 29.
Hermippus, 145.
Herodotus, 140.
Ἥρωες of Timocles, 98.
Herondas, 16, 112 sqq., 123.
Ἥρως of Menander, the, 67, 91, 93, 96.
Hesiod, 7, 100.
Hierocles, 36 sqq.
Hippoclides, 29 n.
Hipponax, 15, 16, 104, 113 sqq.
Hippotherses, Lysias's speech against, 153, 154.
Homer, Anonymous Eulogy on, 57.
Horace, 8.
Hymns, Alexandrian, 110.
    ,, Greek, 41.
    ,, of Callimachus, the, 99.
Hyperides, 116, 155 sqq.
Hyporchema, 42.

Ἴαμβοι of Callimachus, the, 14, 99, 104.
    ,, of Cercidas, 4.
    ,, of Phoenix, 12.
Ibis of Callimachus, the, 99.
Ἱέρεια of Menander, the, 89.
Ἰκάριοι of Timocles, the, 98.
Ἴμβριοι of Menander, the, 89, 90.
Iphigenia of Euripides, the, parodied, 121.
Isocrates, 18, 140.
Isyllus, 46.

Kanarese, 121.
Κανών of Axiopistus, the, 18.
Κιθαριστής of Menander, the, 86, 91, 92.
Κόλαξ of Menander, the, 87, 91, 94.
Κορώνισμα, 13.
Κωνειαζόμεναι of Menander, the, 88, 94.
Kouretes, Hymn of the, 50 sqq.

Λαοδίκειος πόλεμος, 142, 143.
Leonidas of Tarentum, 107.
Limenius, 43 sqq.
Λιθογλύφος of Philemon, the, 98.